*"All the ambassadors in the world and
all the damn wars that have been fought
have in no way come within one thousandth
of the potential of the understanding
that the human race can get from music"*

Sam Phillips
Sun Records
Rock and Roll Producer & Pioneer

Special Thanks

Mick Fleetwood
John Mcvie
Christine Mcvie
Stevie Nicks
Lindsey Buckingham

Rick Turner

Leo Rossi
Jerry Levin
Marc Brickman
And all the Knights of Rock

The Care & Feeding of

Fleetwood Mac

& Other Species

A WILDLIFE GUIDE

Ray Lindsey

TABLE OF CONTENTS

"One good thing about music
When it hits you
You feel no pain"
Trenchtown Rock
Bob Marley

FOREWORD
COMMIT NO NUISANCE

I have worked in the music and sound business for over forty years. I started in the early 1970's before programmable drum machines and auto tune. It was a time when only NASA had lasers and techs. The sound systems were stacked right on the stage and fog machines weren't required to fill the room with smoke.

In 1975 I was hired away from my sound company by Fleetwood Mac to drive a truck for their first tour with new members Stevie Nicks and Lindsey Buckingham. For the next seven years I worked full time as truck driver, equipment guy, stage manager, guitar tuner, accountant, onstage guitar player, electronics guru, caterer, Rastafarian, bartender, chauffeur, security guard, babysitter (child and adult), mechanic and medic. Traditionally known as a roadie. Many came and went but I was the only one besides the faithful Judy Wong who was there full time from beginning to end. It was a rare and supernatural ride void of a game plan. Talent, instinct, and destiny were the driving forces. As the band's success grew, so did the power and chaos. There was an unstoppable energy that fed on itself and continually propelled us forward. Every week was more and bigger. More records sold and more sold out shows. Longer trucks with more equipment for bigger stages. Never-ending months in the studio. Extra buses and nicer planes. More, bigger, longer, and louder was our normal.

This was the beginning of the golden age of the business of live rock and roll and the early years of large scale tour production. There was a lot of money to be made playing in sports arenas and football stadiums. A new business model was inspiring long-haired innovators and entrepreneurs to elevate the aesthetics of live music events. This was done while raking in huge piles of partially accounted for cash. Creativity, commerce, and the counterculture merged and clamored for a hip place on the grid. Fleetwood Mac landed right in the middle of this uncharted territory. They survived and succeeded the only way they knew how—on their own terms.

Between 1992 and 2009 I worked exclusively for Lindsey Buckingham. We recorded a number of albums in his home studio and embarked on numerous solo tours. Lindsey was often asked in interviews to compare those efforts to Fleetwood Mac and was fond of calling one the "small machine" and the other the "big machine." In May of 1975 when I started with the band, Fleetwood Mac was a very small machine but their signature sound and musicality was already apparent. Forty years later the band has assembled their largest machine ever. As the group and their fans celebrate the return of Christine McVie to the stage, I am warmed with the memories of the early days and simpler times. Without the great Peter Green, there would never have been a Fleetwood Mac, but for me, the five musicians who made up the band in 1975 were the defining formation of the group. No producer, manager, lawyer, or floors of accountants could have put them together. In spite of the countless emotions that drive them apart, the band couldn't, and still can't, deny the musical magnetism that keeps them playing together. I was immersed in a potent and enticing stew that was too compelling for a sheltered kid from the Midwest to walk away from. I made myself a safe place in the eye of the storm keeping all of the band's toys working and accounted for. I acquired miles of rope while avoiding to hang myself with it. In addition, I also played guitar on stage with the band for every show between 1977 and 1982.

A lot of international attention has been stirred up by the enormous success of the band's recent reunion. Their colorful history and survival instincts are recounted in the media worldwide. When a *LIFE* magazine reporter contacted me for background information for the publication's tribute to the band, his first question to me was,

"How do you become a roadie for Fleetwood Mac?" John McVie's answer would be that I must have lost a bet but there's a lot more to it than that.

"Hey, leave the guy alone, He's got his soldering iron and he makes me sound good and he can drive the truck."

Pete Townshend

CHAPTER 1
TERRY AND GLORIA

I was born in Newport, Rhode Island to Terry and Gloria Lindsey. My dad was in the Navy and my mom brought me into the world at the base hospital. I was a reluctant arrival and made my first appearance with black eyes from the forceps the doctor clamped on my head to assist in my entrance. After pop's hitch was up we moved to Wichita, Kansas where his dad, Ray Ralph, was hooked up with the aircraft industry. Both my folks were seeking distance from their kinfolk in the hills of central Ohio and our little trio shared a fresh start in the easygoing wheat fields of the Midwest. Roots were established and careers were born as my folks took on the adventures of young parenthood in the 1950's. Wichita is known as the "Air Capital."It's a reference to the numerous aviation industries that make their home there. Wichita is also deep in the fabric of the "Great Plains." It's windy and hot in the summer and windy and cold in the winter. A table flat prairie extends five hundred miles west to Denver as the elevation imperceptibly rises from one thousand three hundred feet to a mile above sea level.

I grew up in the middle of Middle America. My childhood was a Huck Finn and Ray Bradbury world with an extra scoop of conservative. A buckle on the Bible Belt and home to The John Birch Society, Wichita was very comfortable with the straight and narrow. All in all, I was a happy kid. It was a time and a place where you could safely walk to school, take a swim in the river, and ride your bike until bedtime. Terry and Gloria worked their asses off to make a safe and cozy home. Dad would play catch with me after work while my mom cooked us supper. After dinner we would play Monopoly or Scrabble and in the summer, we would sit on the front porch and listen to Harry Caray's play-by-play announcing of the St. Lois Cardinals.

The Lindsey's 1958

One of my earliest memories of the presence of a higher power was the smell and feel of the summer storms that would slowly creep in until black clouds filled the sky. Out of nowhere the temperature would drop thirty degrees while the wind bent trees and rattled screen doors. About the time the barometer bottomed out and the lightning started, rain would be pounding and thunder rolling. Sometimes these systems had tornadoes in them and the sirens would send us all scrambling to the shelters. The exhilaration of invading storms coupled with being scared shitless provided an excellent adrenalin bump for all the shiny children of the Plains.

By the time I was eight I was bespectacled with buckteeth and big ears. I loved baseball, basketball, and music. Terry played trombone and I would sit next to him in the garage and listen to him jazz out. Soon I was playing trumpet in the school band. We spent a lot of quality time in that garage. Besides rebuilding the engine in our Oldsmobile, Dad tore down and reassembled piece by piece an old upright piano. Both the car and piano found new life. The car stayed outside and the piano was promoted to a residence in the living room. Dad's piano style leaned towards ragtime and old standards. We had a Silvertone stereo with the tilt down turntable and a selection of LP's that included Frank Sinatra, Al Hirt, Herb Alpert, and Floyd Kramer as well as show tunes and Big Band music.

My first box of electronics was a tiny transistor radio and I loved it but wasn't buying into early sixties pop. I was a nine-year-old jazz snob. Linda Tilton, my across the street neighbor and babysitter, was a regular teenage American girl obsessed with the Beatles and I didn't get it. I was already developing a bad attitude towards anything that smelled of trendy. On Christmas Eve of 1964 I had to confront my bias toward the band from Liverpool. The Pierce kids, my little brother Bobby, and myself were dropped off at a matinee so our overworked parents could finish their holiday shopping. I was already vibrating from the anticipation of gift-opening coupled with the surprise of an afternoon movie. Coca Cola and a box of Raisinets fueled my buzz and I was starting to peak when the opening chord of *A Hard Day's Night* came soaring out of the Orpheum's Altec sound system. This was my first time hearing rock music being delivered from high decibel high fidelity speakers. I was elated and mesmerized by the guitars, drums, and harmonies. The big sound was a physical and emotional wave that slammed into me. It messed me up in a very good way. For ninety minutes I forgot about Christmas and got my first glimpse of a grown-up and hip world beyond the Air Capital. When the movie was over, we walked outside to falling snow and Christmas carolers singing on the sidewalk. *Joy to the World.* I was sublime.

The excitement of Christmas reclaimed my emotions and for a few days I was lost in all the distractions that the season brought. No homework, lots of food and new gadgets to take apart. Too soon, the newness of my presents wore off and the dread of back to school returned. I didn't want the good stuff to end. I wanted to feel the feelings I had when I first heard the sound of those guitars through the big speakers on Christmas Eve. I took my Xmas stocking five dollar bill and bought *Beatles '65.* This was the first album of mine to find a place in the record rack with my parents LP's.

As rock and roll began to gain ground in my body and our house, I started to look closer at the boxes all this sacred sound was coming out of. When I discovered the electric pen from my wood burning set was really a soldering iron, I entered a new phase of electronic disassembly and modification. I added extension speakers to my AM/FM clock radio and installed a headphone jack on the family record player. The ham radio guy at the electronics shop sold me a stereo quarter-inch jack and showed me how to wire it so the speakers would disengage when headphones were inserted. Most of my summer lawn-mowing money was laid out to buy a pair of Koss headphones. Initially this project was intended to spare my parents from the unsettling sounds that their eldest child was becoming obsessed with. I was a good kid. I wasn't trying to be unpleasant to live with but something was getting a hold on me and wasn't letting go. When I heard for the first time what stereo really sounded like through my headphones, I was seriously blown away. I loved listening to music. The pure beauty of just listening. The intimacy and solitude was such a wonderful place to be. I was spiraling out of audio control in a sensible and non-rebellious way.

By the time I made it to junior high, I was listening to Woody Guthrie, Bob Dylan, The Kingston Trio, and all things folkie. Simon and Garfunkel albums sounded great on the headphones. Acoustic finger-picking was calling me and I started a search for my own guitar. Victor Worth was my next-door neighbor and tolerated me hanging around while he worked on his car with his friends. In his bedroom was a bottom of the line Sears acoustic guitar that he would let me bang around on. Sensing Vic was more mechanic than musician, I offered him the rest of my summer lawn-mowing money for the dusty six string. Fifteen dollars later I was cradling my first guitar and pondering which corner of my bedroom it should live.

In the tradition of all low-end beginner guitars, it was nearly impossible to play. If you could get through the first month of callus building, you could move on to actually learning a song. I was pretty much on my own as far figuring out what to do. School band had taught me how to read music so I bought *MelBay's Guitar for Beginners* and got a hold of a Bob Dylan songbook. Like most introverted adolescent boys, I valued my alone time and teaching myself to play was a good reason to stay in my room with the door closed. I worked that crappy little guitar over with my handful of folk chords for the duration of junior high.

High school was my time to start stepping out. I began playing guitar in public and got into school theatre. I was comfortable on stage but wasn't that good. I became increasingly interested in the microphones and speakers and was always trying to figure out how to make things sound less crappy.

The spring of 1971 was my junior year at Wichita High School East and student elections were in full swing. The prom royalty / student council traditions were losing their luster in the politically conscious early seventies. They were seen as a club for the school elite who went to their own dances and attended their own meetings. There were fundraisers to finance the social events and committees formed to discuss the budgets of next years parties. All in all, a pretty self-sufficient cartel that the rest of the school coexisted with.

Posters for the upcoming student elections were starting to appear in the hallways. Predictable slogans in glue, glitter, and magic marker filled the walls. Anne Harlenske was running for senior class president. A sweet girl with all the credentials, Anne had been on every student council since seventh grade. This final coronation was her destiny, but the pronouncement on her campaign poster was just too enticing. It demanded a response.

"Anne Can!"

Her posters were everywhere and every time I saw one all I could I think of was "Ray May..."

Soon "Ray May..." posters randomly appeared next to "Anne Can!" posters throughout the school.

I was satisfied that I had achieved my goal of throwing a satirical hand grenade into the works. However, when the administration came calling, they explained to me the need for adherence to school protocol. Posters for the upcoming election were allowed for candidates only. Unless I intended to run for an office, they would need to come down. My good humored politically aware friend, Chuck Campbell, took this information as a challenge and pressed me to take it up a notch. After discovering only one person was running for senior class president and one for student body president, he convinced me it was our democratic duty to step up and not allow them to run unopposed. We MUST stand up for the system! The next day our hats were thrown into the ring along with the real kids. With no agenda and signage already posted, our campaigns were low key. There wasn't a chance of beating the incumbents and we were never serious about winning to begin with. It was more like performance art. In a couple of weeks, the joke had run it's course. All that was left was our election day speech in front of the student body. Chuck was first and proceeded to scare the adults with a Hunter Thompson style tirade that referenced Abbie Hoffman and other current lefties. He wore green fatigues, army boots, and a jungle field cap. With his impressive beard, he took on the persona of a long lost relative of Fidel Castro. Even satirical references to communism in early seventies Wichita were met with apprehension and raising of the eyebrows. Many of the faculty took him to be totally serious and were concerned. Freaked out, actually. The student body did not sense the same foreboding and were amused. My speech was more on the warm and fuzzy side. Portraying a caricature of the consummate smarmy politician, I promised the incoming senior class every creature comfort I could think of. Of course, if elected, I would have no power whatsoever to fulfill any of my promises. We had a great time. It was all very over the top and good clean fun. A landslide victory for our competitors was assured.

The next day election results came in. Due to the entertainment value, twice as many students voted than in previous elections. The people spoke and Chuck won by five votes and I won by three. There was considerable displeasure in the front office. Multiple recounts of the vote delayed the final announcement for days. The administration finally conceded and made it official. Chuck Campbell, Student Body President; Ray Lindsey, Senior Class President. What a mess. First, this was absolutely not what we planned or even thought possible. We were not student council material nor did we want to be. We also felt bad for our rivals, Roger and Anne. None of this was personal. We were up front about our tongues being firmly planted in our cheeks. This was their sacred world and we pissed on it. They were genuinely hurting over the results. The powers that be were fearing unrest in the classrooms. The school's social elite were REALLY mad at us. A hard lesson was learned. Do not fuck with politics.

There was eventually a happy ending. Summer vacation came and went and it was time for back to school. Hurt feelings were soothed and fences were mended. Basically, Chuck and I appointed all the kids that usually ran things to be in charge of all the stuff we didn't care about. Balance was restored and peace prevailed in the halls. The only real power we had was organizing fundraisers. We put on a concert of local folkies in the school auditorium and sold tickets to raise money for the class coffers. No profit was realized as I spent the few dollars we made on a good sound system—I knew our school P.A. sucked because I had been coddling it for two years. My first presentation as a promoter was not going to be tainted with shitty audio. I contracted the only local company with rock credentials, Superior Sound, and everyone enjoyed a major upgrade in sound quality. The show was an artistic success but a fundraising bust.

Graduation spared my alma mater any further political distress. I spent my first summer of freedom playing guitar and being in love with my first real girlfriend, Sally Patton. Three months of bliss crashed to the ground on Labor Day when my baby left for Dallas to continue her education at SMU. Since I had nothing to live for, I enrolled in three classes at the local citadel of higher education, Wichita State. That lasted six weeks. After five months of self-pity and delivering flowers to hospitals and funeral homes, I hit bottom and began the healing process of searching my soul for my true path.

Superior Sound on Central was ground zero for the sparse hippie community of students from Wichita State University. Jim Pearce and Brock Jabara were owners and operators of the only high-end high volume audio gear in Kansas and the surrounding states. Brock was the engineer/designer and Jim cooked the books. In the summer, free concerts with local bands were put together on Sunday afternoons in bucolic Riverside Park. The P.A. was always provided by Superior Sound. This struck me as a noble and vital profession. First there was the social component. It wasn't really a party until the big sound was turned on. And there was the nerd component—an overwhelming collection of speakers, amplifiers, and cables that needed tending by men with compassion and vision. Perhaps there was a place for me amongst the boxes and wires.

CHAPTER 2
FINNIGAN AND WOOD

It was another miserable grey Wichita winter. The already anemic local music scene was barely breathing. I felt like a trapped badger with no way out. My only relief was the occasional visiting rock shows but they were a cruel tease. Once a month, touring bands would stop at Henry Levitt Arena for a day and disappear again.

And so, with no plan whatsoever, I drove to the little shop on Central to engage the proprietors of Superior Sound. Perhaps they knew of the way out of town. At the curb in front, co-owner Jim Pearce was loading black wooden cases into a white van. Thirty minutes and forty boxes later, a seedling of an escape was sown. Jim's wife had bailed at the last minute and there was an open seat available for the trip to the college town of Lawrence, KS. Finnigan and Wood were playing that night at the Red Dog Inn and Superior Sound was the audio vendor. For no money and a couple of hamburgers, I was offered the opportunity to drive a van, carry a bunch of heavy boxes in and out of a Kansas bar and drive back home. I wasted no time taking the shotgun position next to Jim.

Mike Finnigan is blessed with a golden blues voice and over the top R&B keyboard skills. He is Ray Charles and Jimmy Smith in a tall white man's body. Mr. Finnigan was well known in the Midwest from his bands in the sixties, The Serfs and The Jerry Hahn Brotherhood. He also played the Hammond B-3 on the legendary Jimi Hendrix album, *Electric Ladyland.* His new band, Finnigan and Wood, were touring in his adopted home state of Kansas in support of their new album, *Crazed Hipsters.* Mike's local popularity was so strong that the other bars in town would close the night they were playing and redirect their patrons to the chosen venue. Events of this caliber were rare in the flatlands and the folks who were tuned in packed every bar and roadhouse the band played at. The Red Dog in Lawrence was THE spot for the University of Kansas coeds, hippies and jocks. Packed to it's sixty year old rafters, the club patrons and myself were treated to a night of full force R&B rock and soul. In my sedate eighteen years alive in the heartland I had never seen, heard or felt a party of this magnitude. It was a game changer and an eye opener. I had been to lots of concerts and seen some really good shows but this was a night the likes of which I had not known to exist. I had witnessed the divine power of a great live band coupled with a full house of true believers.

Jim and I loaded the truck after the show and drove the three hours back to Wichita. It was four a.m. by the time we got the gear back in the shop. I was tired but still buzzing. Jim said there was another show that night in Salina if I wanted to tag along. He told me to come back around two and I could help him pack the truck. I was back to the shop by ten a.m. and proceeded to interrogate Jim and Brock about everything they did until it was time to take off.

The venue in Salina, KS was a little lower on the elegance ladder than the Red Dog and a more typical example of Midwest watering holes. Finnigan affectionately referred to these gigs as "upholstered sewers." The casual aesthetics did not diminish the enthusiasm of the crowd. The exit doors were propped open to the parking lot as there were as many patrons outside as inside. We were not burdened with formalities like fire codes and occupancy limits. There was one guy at the door and he was "security." My all access pass was a microphone cable in my hand.

For a month, I was a tent show roustabout. We did three or four shows a week all over the state and would drive home every night after each show. Every single gig was oversold and over the top. I was in teenage hippie heaven soaking up a rock and roll internship. I got fed and in return did whatever was needed. Brock was happy to train me in the ways of traveling sound systems so he could stay home with his wife and new baby. When the Midwest leg of the tour was completed, the circus left town and headed back to California. I was back in Wichita with no job but had witnessed the holy spirit and had no plans to backslide.

Finnigan and Wood

Jim and Brock had been doing their thing in Wichita for a few years and were big ducks in a small pond. Five-week tours like Finnigan and Wood were rare. Most of their business was local one-offs and none of that made much money. Brock was always prototyping projects they could build and sell in quantity. Before his Galaxy HotSpot monitors took off, the boys found another way to generate consistent income. Consistent income was good because it meant I might actually get paid.

Chance Manufacturing was a Wichita-based company that built traveling amusement park rides for the county fair circuit. Traditionally, ride operators used bullhorns to entice fairgoers to buy tickets for their attraction. Looking to upgrade the old methods of attention-grabbing, the company reached out to Brock to design a portable sound system that would stir up the young and disappearing seventies crowd. Superior Sound joined the carnival ride business and I became a one-man assembly line.

Brock taught me how to read schematics and solder like a NASA technician. I assembled all the electronics in one room and went next door to the wood shop to turn sheets of plywood into speaker cabinets. It was a one-stop trade school AND I was getting paid. My opening wage was fifty dollars a week. I lived in the back of the wood shop and Jim's wife, Barbara, fed me dinner. On weekends I was either mixing sound for local shows or playing guitar in the neighborhood bars. Life was good in a self-sufficient hippie kind of way but I couldn't shake the memories of my brief brush with the higher power. I felt the pond shrinking around me and time slipping away. After a year, I got the urge for going and a stranger from California led the way.

CHAPTER 3
TYCOBRAHE

The late sixties was the beginning of rock and roll getting LOUD. Groups didn't travel with their own P.A.'s and it was the responsibility of the promoter putting on the show to supply lights and sound. That meant visiting bands usually played through a public address system that was twenty years old and screwed to the wall. This gear was usually adequate for commencement speeches and school plays. This led to a new school of promoters who understood the value of creating a performing and listening environment that was pleasing to musicians and audiences. Venues like the Grande Ballroom in Detroit and Bill Graham's Fillmores in San Francisco and New York were as famous for their house sound as they were their ambience. Every happening band wanted to play where the sound was good.

In Los Angeles the place to be was Exposition Hall adjacent to the Shrine Auditorium. Leased by Pinnacle Dance Concerts, this company would eventually morph into Pacific Presentations and later Avalon Attractions. A big factor in their early success was their custom sound system. Designed by studio engineer John Judnich, it utilized audiophile components that were powerful and compact. JBL loaded speaker cabinets were driven by high-end MacIntosh hi-fi amps and mixing was through a studio recording console. They used this system for The Buffalo Springfield, The Grateful Dead, Jefferson Airplane, Country Joe and the Fish, Moby Grape, Janis Joplin, BB King, Albert King, Taj Mahal, Jimi Hendrix, The Yardbirds, Junior Wells, Buddy Guy, John Mayall, Jeff Beck, Rod Stewart, Pink Floyd, Cream, The

Electric Flag, Traffic, Fleetwood Mac, The Who, The Doors and Love, and so on.

A rained out festival at the Rose Bowl found the partners short on cash and the sound gear was handed over to investor Bob Bogdanovich to cover his losses. Bob took engineer Judnich and started Tycobrahe Sound. From there, Bob aligned his forces with audio engineer/ designer extraordinaire Jim Gamble.

Bob Bogdanovich and his original P.A.

Jim grew up in Southern California and started doing sound at surfer gigs in 1958. He had an old Hudson with a huge backseat and put two of his homebuilt speakers in there. He didn't do the P.A. for the bands, he just played records when they stopped to make some money for hamburgers. At that time bands were still plugging their high impedance microphones into their guitar amps. When Dick Dale came along, he told Jim, "I want to sing through your shit because it sounds better than my shit." Dick's vocal mic was plugged in and immediately blew out all the speakers.

Jim joined the Navy in the mid-sixties and took advantage of the U.S. government's fine electronics training programs. After his stint in the service, he returned to college for more high-end circuitry courses.

He also played bass with an up and coming West Coast band and went on tour supporting their record.

After a short run of club gigs, it became painfully obvious that this was no way to make a living or pursue a career. As Jim told Art Thompson in Stompbox in 1997:

"I started my sound business right then in 1969. That's when Bob Bogdanovich came along. Bob was a college kid who just stumbled into the audio business. His father was really rich. He owned StarKist Tuna and half of the Heinz Corporation. Bob got some money from his dad and gave it to the promoters for Civic Presentations who were putting on a gig at the Rose Bowl. They had done a bunch of other gigs and made lots of money, but this time it rained and nobody came. They lost their shirts. The only thing they had left was their P.A. system. They gave it to Bob who just put it in his garage. Then the weather got nice and people started saying "Hey, break that shit out and let's have a party at Griffith Park." So Bob started doing free shows there for all the big bands. Pretty soon they started hiring him. I had my own sound company and I was bidding against him for shows around the area. One day we did a Frank Zappa show at Exposition Hall and we put both systems together. Bob liked the sound and suggested we keep it that way. I thought "Great, there go all my new mics.""

"That's how it happened. We just kind of joined up. Later, a couple of other crazy fuckers got involved. They went around stuffing cocaine up everybody's noses to get gigs and we started gigging. Bob got the name from the Danish astronomer who was wrong about everything. Tyco Brahe thought the planets revolved around the earth and had a gold nose because his had been bitten off. It was the perfect name for Bob's company. The swirly logo that went around the name came from a mortuary ad that he saw on a bus stop bench.

"We started making amps and speakers and mixers back when nothing was any good. It was all Altec tube shit. We built transistor amps before Crown. We were doing sound for everybody. Fleetwood Mac, Uriah Heap, ELO, Savoy Brown, Deep Purple, Black Sabbath, Jethro Tull, Rod Stewart, the Stones—most of the English second wave of bands."

Bob was still tight with all of his boys from Pacific Presentations and they worked together to put a business face on this rock and roll touring thing. Tycobrahe was THE Southern California sound system preferred by anybody playing in the LA area. Promoter and sound vendor linked together for a mutually advantageous partnership.

Bands headlining for Pacific Presentations would have their audio needs handled by Tycobrahe and as the promoter supplying production support, Pacific would pay Bob for his gear. Everyone made money and the bands were always happy.

This win-win business model took Tycobrahe to the next level of tour support logistics. Amplifiers, speakers, and mixing consoles were all manufactured in-house in Hermosa Beach and all of their touring systems were identical. White Tycobrahe trucks fanned out regionally across the country and picked up the shows of the band's that requested their hardware. A single system with a two-man crew might have a week of shows in a three or four state area. One night with the Faces, two with Black Sabbath, and two more with Ten Years After. The bands knew that whatever system they met up with would all work and sound the same. The bulk of English bands touring in the early seventies supported this approach to P.A. rental and Tycobrahe was very busy for many years.

By 1974, Tycobrahe had five systems on the road. On Saturday, April 6 they combined the touring packages of Black Oak Arkansas, Deep Purple, Black Sabbath, Rare Earth, and Earth, Wind and Fire for the first California Jam. Also on the bill was Seals and Crofts, the Eagles, and Emerson, Lake and Palmer. The one-day festival drew two hundred and fifty thousand paying fans and set a record for the loudest amplification system ever installed. This represented another milestone in the growing up of the rock business. Woodstock may have drawn more people but only a few thousand actually bought tickets. The California Jam generated the highest gross in rock history up to that time. The show was produced by ABC television in partnership with Pacific Presentations and was shown on the network's In Concert series. The audio portion of the show was also broadcast in stereo on FM radio. For the partying paying public, thousands of drinking fountains and toilets were installed as well as access to a forty-five-bed hospital constructed in the infield.

Every act except ELP performed on a stage that supported two separate decks that moved in and out on a railroad track. As one act played, the next one set their gear and was ready to roll into position without any downtime between bands. Emerson, Lake and Palmer were the co-headliners with Deep Purple and closed the show. The English progressive rock powerhouse was the current leader in over the top theatrics and were set up on their own dedicated stage. This was needed to accommodate the structure required to fly their Steinway grand piano twenty feet in the air and spin it end over end with keyboardist Keith Emerson strapped to the bench.

Tycobrahe's engineers along with Pacific Presentations worked months prior to the show anticipating the audio complexities of a production this size. Prevailing winds had been studied and the stage was positioned to take audio advantage of their predicted patterns. Putting on a rock festival is one thing but making it TV compatible adds extra layers of potential technical complications. The single largest audio issue was integrating the house and monitor electronics with the Wally Heider recording truck and the ABC broadcast unit. All audio to every destination was rendered hum-free with a custom-built Tycobrahe mic splitter that utilized multi-tap transformers for each input. The technology required wasn't groundbreaking but anticipating and preparing for the potential buzz fest was an example of the clear-eyed adult thinking that was creeping into the live music business. There were also cultural conflicts to overcome. Rock musicians were not interested in compatibility with television production values. Going back to the early days of radio, broadcasting relied on military-based protocol and nomenclature. Scheduling was tracked to the second and sticking to the script was a given. Even though these sensibilities were shunned by the performers, the careful planning by promoter and sound company neutralized most anarchy.

Multiple band all-day shows were famously not-on-time affairs. Running late and behind schedule was all part of the fun. Co-headliners Deep Purple had negotiated to play next to last before Emerson, Lake and Palmer. The band had reasoned that once you factored in being two to three hours behind schedule, they would actually hit the stage at the prime time of the night and get out of there before the audience started losing steam. In a rock festival first, not only was the Jam not three hours late, it was right on time. The producers on the TV side of the camp were very impressed with themselves for running a tight ship but their remaining artists were not. Deep Purple was being forced to take the stage with a late afternoon sun still blazing on the horizon—a headliner buzz kill of great proportion. The band and their manager locked themselves in their trailer and refused to come out until twilight settled in. The director and his staff demanded compliance and the Deep Purple camp replied with a hearty "fuck off." Animosity soured the good vibes and when the band did finally emerge, they were not to be messed with. Fireworks, explosives, amplifiers in flames and a guitar rammed into a sixty thousand-dollar ABC Wide World of Sports camera were some of the debris left by the provoked English band

and crew. The kids loved it. ABC did not. Rock and Roll was not yet TV friendly. It would be awhile before these two opposing forces of entertainment nature would find a way to coexist.

One month after the California Jam, Bob Bogdanovich parked his bobtail in front of my friend's little sound company in Wichita and borrowed me to help him clean up and repair the P.A. in his truck. At the end of the day I offered my services for any work he might have in the future. Two weeks later I was flying to Chicago to do my first show for Tycobrahe Sound.

CHAPTER 4
NOT IN KANSAS ANYMORE

Bob picked me up in front of baggage claim at Chicago's O'Hare airport in the same eighteen-foot white bobtail truck that I helped load in Wichita two weeks previous. He put me behind the wheel and gave me some pointers on shifting a ten-speed. We headed towards downtown Chicago with gears a grinding. I had never driven a truck this size before but that was of little concern to Bob. He was totally fine giving me the time to sort it out. I soon learned that this was his mentoring style. As long as I was willing take something on he was content giving me as much as I could handle. He never made me feel uncomfortable. His manner was neither patronizing or particularly supportive. It was more like we got a job to do and here's how it needs to be done. I would find out later that Bob wasn't that excited about music or concerts. I don't think he cared much for musicians either.

What Bob did know how to do was talk to anybody, anywhere, anytime and get them to give him whatever he needed. This was the only time I saw him enjoying himself. He treated every stagehand, taxi driver, promoter, and bartender the same. He would engage an individual, explain what he wanted from them and then let them know the best way they could accomplish meeting his needs. It was a gift. He was honest and respectful but seemed to be wishing he was anywhere else but at a rock show. He would also take every opportunity to point out to me the futility of trusting anyone associated with show business.

These were the lessons of his ancient wisdom that were passed on to me. Besides showing me one time how to assemble his company's sound system, we had no other discussions about the nuances of professional audio protocol. He was not a fan of nerdy technical chit chat. The show in Chicago featured Dave Mason and Golden Earring. After an afternoon sound check, Bob said I should mix the show. This was a bold and brave offer from the guy who owned the top sound company in the country. All he knew about me was that I was an eager hayseed hippie kid who could barely shift a ten-speed. I sensed a pattern developing. Another toss in the deep end. Who was this guy?

The Auditorium Theatre was one of the nicest places to play in Chicago. Our system sounded good in there and I was thrilled/scared to death to be handed the keys to the console. By the time the show started, I was a buzzing bag of adrenalin. Bob hung out for a couple of songs and disappeared for the rest of the night. Nothing blew up so I felt pretty good about my piloting skills. At the end of the night Bob reappeared and gave me his heartfelt critique of my maiden voyage. His review was brief. "Let's get this shit out of here." And so we did.

Two weeks later back in Wichita, I got the call to fly out and meet Mr. Bogdonavich in St. Louis, MO. It was the same travel scenario as before. A prepaid ticket in my name would be waiting for me at the airport. Parked in front of baggage claim of Lambert Field was the familiar white Tycobrahe truck. Feeling cocky I offered to drive. Next stop was Keil Auditorium in the declining downtown of a once great riverboat city. The theatre was well known and well used. Another union house but without the edge and crankiness of the Chicago local. Instead of surly, the stagehands were just old. I triumphantly backed our truck into position on the first try and pretended that I always did it that way. We opened the rolling door and I stepped back to let Bob start running the show. Instead, he hands the keys back to me and says, "I've got to find a phone and make some calls. Set up our gear and get this shit working." And, once again, he was gone.

I looked at my team of graying card-carrying theatrical stage workers and asked myself "What would Bob do?" I quickly made friends with the crew chief and proceeded to engage the troops "Bob" style. I delegated, placated, and anticipated. You needed to keep everybody busy and not lose anyone in the process. Sometimes there are wanderers that can disappear completely all day and magically reappear at night in time to turn in their timecards. Self deprecating humor and a keen eye was useful in keeping the natives local.

One of the strengths of the Tycobrahe design was the packaging of all the components. "Roadieproof" was the philosophy of creating minimal assembly points and utilizing one-way only multi-pin connectors. This steered road weary sound men away from implementing system-killing set up errors. The entire P.A. could be up and running in an hour. My first time took three hours with the St. Louie stage crew but it all worked so I was pretty satisfied. I spooled up ZZ Top on the Revox 2 track and enjoyed the aural fruits of my labors. I had five minutes of self-satisfied reflection when Bob reappeared with news. He handed me a three by five notecard. On it was the name and address of a venue in Denver. Underneath that was the phone number of Bob's office in Hermosa Beach. He informed me that he's leaving for the airport and I would be on my own. I am to finish this show up, load out and drive eight hundred miles to Denver for a show two days later. He said he would try to meet me there but to set up without him. More importantly, I needed to collect our fee from tonight's promoter before the show. No matter what I was told, I was to not under any circumstances turn on the P.A. until the cash was in my pocket. He told me to get receipts for everything I spent and was gone. Bob wasn't big on long goodbyes.

The one and only act that evening was Al Green. I loved Al Green. I grew up on R&B and soul music. His records were at the top of both the soul and pop charts and he was a god in the black community. Al's style is smooth, funky, soulful, sexy, romantic. His band was as Memphis-sweet as it gets. I was looking forward to being in the presence of greatness.

The band showed up and started putting their stage gear together. I had labeled and plugged in my mics already and just needed to finish placing them. Time to get paid.

I found the promoter in a tiny office just off the stage. Two African American brothers the size of linebackers moved in between me and a desk piled with cash. A serious but friendly well dressed black man sat behind the desk and introduced himself as the promoter. He said Bob told him I would be stopping by for the payment for the sound system and asked "How much was that again?"

"Seven hundred and fifty." I replied.

He said "I can give you five hundred now and you can pick up the rest after the show."

I couldn't believe it. This cordial and stylish man was trying to fuck me and seeing if I would fall for it. I looked at the promoter. I looked at the line backers. I looked at the thousands of dollars on the desk in front of me. Through the door I could hear the unmistakable snap of Al Jackson Jr.'s snare drum. The band was starting the show without me.

I'm thinking Bob was totally capable of setting this all up. I'm also thinking I'm really outnumbered. I sat down between the two large chaperones and proceeded to unreel the story of my entire day finishing with Bob's instructions about when I could turn the sound on. I was going to be fired before I even got hired. The crowd let out a roar and magically all seven hundred and fifty dollars was counted and stacked in front of me. I reached out to capture the booty when a gigantic black hand appeared and and landed on the pile of cash. I looked up at the owner of the massive mitt. He handed me the money and said, "Better make it sound good or we're taking this back." Everybody had a good laugh while the bug-eyed skinny kid sprinted back to the stage.

The band was already playing and the nine thousand-seat room was packed. The front third of the floor seats were filled with women holding huge bouquets of roses. I had already turned the microphones on and could hear the sound in the room build as I put them in place. First the kick drum then the snare and high hat. After the drums I got the bass and guitar in. By the time I got to the horns the band was in full flight. I set Al's vocal mic and headed out to the mix position in the audience.

The band was playing Al's intro just as I arrived at my console. Mr. Green strolled on stage and was bombarded with twenty rows of roses. The entire stage was a foot deep in crimson flowers. All the females in the theatre were either crying or screaming. It was unbe-lievable. The P.A. and band sounded great. Sometimes as a mixer, there are days when your job is all about damage control. It could be a bad band, bad acoustics, bad gear, or just a bad day but you had to make the best of what you had and get over it. This was not one of those nights. After five minutes, the sound was on cruise control. I had learned when I worked for Count Basie the value of keeping it simple and not overthinking the task at hand. A great band will find the way to their comfort zone and let the music do the heavy lifting. I was a lone shiny white face in a sea of St. Louis brothers and sisters attending services in the Church of Reverend Al Green. The real deal is the real deal and there wasn't a non-believer in the room. Everyone stayed on their feet all the way through the last encore. At the end, the house lights came up and the satisfied crowd returned to the steamy St. Louis summer night outside. Once again, I was by myself.

Miraculously, all of my stagehands returned for load out and an hour later I was headed west on Interstate 70 with more cash in my pocket than I had ever seen in my life. It would seem I had passed my audition.

CHAPTER 5
THIS AIN'T THE SUMMER OF LOVE

The Blue Oyster Cult was Long Island's answer to Black Sabbath minus Ozzie. Diminutive in stature and large in attitude, BOC filled arenas with a heavy metal barrage of sound cloaked in mysterious darkness. With black leather, chains, and and a fondness for science fiction they kept their fans agitated and entertained. In June 1974, I joined up with the mollusk—worshipping quintet for my first tour with Tycobrahe Sound.

I landed in Greensboro, North Carolina after a day of flying and cabbed to the Coliseum. The show had already started and opening band Lynyrd Skynyrd was onstage. Two of their guitar players were engaged in a fist fight while the third was finishing his guitar solo. Empty and half-filled Jack Daniels bottles littered the deck. The audience and the band were equally inebriated and it was a rowdy scene. When Blue Oyster Cult took the stage, fights continued in the audience. The only cops there were at the front doors and didn't seem to be interested in crowd control. Rock shows always have a few loose cannons but this was the worst I had ever seen. Large-scale fucked up with little or no adult supervision. After a few songs, BOC pummeled the downer-induced faithful into submission and the show finished up with minimal hostility. We loaded out, stuffed seven guys and their luggage into a van and I began my first big time rock tour.

Blue Oyster Cult logo

As the new guy, I kept a low profile and soaked up everything I could about this new and intriguing social situation. We played five or six shows a week through the South and up the East Coast and I was seeing a wide variety of music from our opening bands. In the South where BOC was working to expand their fan base, promoters would often group us with southern rock boogie bands to mixed results. When we got back to Blue Oyster turf in the Northeast the opening acts were the NY Dolls (my first exposure to men wearing makeup and heels) and Kiss (my only time to have stage blood vomited into my monitors). It was game on and our audiences were a force to be reckoned with. Most of the stages were only four or five feet high and there were no barriers to keep a defensible space between patron and performer. Every show was a nightlong cat and mouse game between myself and any number of toasted dudes grabbing cables and pulling the attached microphone into the crowd. Since I was financially responsible for every hundred dollar Shure SM57 mic that was lost, it was my duty to jump in and retrieve our property. No one had any intention of keeping or stealing our stuff. It was just a fun way to kill time while the crew was setting up the next band. Ironically, the hippies working onstage were viewed as authority figures deserving of being fucked with. In the kids' eyes, we were the man and it was their duty to stick it to us. This was mostly just a pain in the ass and had always been harmless until the night my partner jumped in and was stabbed in the belly as I pulled him back in. From that point on, all excursions into the crowd were done in teams and with a mic stand for self defense.

It wasn't all mindless mayhem. The guys in the band were amiable hipsters who could whip up a convincing noise with a sense of humor. Presaging Spinal Tap, every show had a number where all five guys strapped on an axe and lined up on the front of the stage for a guitar army massacre. The kids loved it.

We played in every type of venue from arenas to roller rinks. You never knew what you were going to get until you rolled up. Engel Stadium in Chatanooga, Tennessee was a baseball park built in 1930 and was once a jewel of the South. Those glory days had long since passed and all that was left were rundown bleachers and a dirt lot where an emerald field of green grass once thrived. In the center of the ancient sod a four-foot high wooden stage had been built and that was it. No roof, no backstage, no barriers or fences anywhere. A lone outhouse behind the stage stood next to a power pole with a transformer on top and a breaker box on the bottom. This was the entirety of our facility for the day. We backed the truck up to the plywood platform and got on with the task of getting the day over with. It was a daytime show and with any luck we would get this done by dinner time.

A crowd of four or five thousand were already in the park and were wasting no time getting wasted. We rolled everything straight on the deck, tied our tails into the power pole and got some music going. A local blues band opened with a shuffle and were halfway through their first song when the transformer at the top of the porta pottie pole exploded. The P.A. made a sound like a death rattle as our only source of power went up in flames. This was the first time the promoter responsible for this elegant gathering made his appearance.

He demanded to have the sound turned back on. He struggled to make the connection between the power failure and our inability to continue with his well appointed show. The second act on the bill were regional favorites Larry Raspberry and the Highsteppers. A full-on super tight R&B show band from Memphis, the Highsteppers were close friends with the local show runner and offered a possible solution. Larry's singer and wife, Carol, was a former Miss Tennessee and was friends with the state's governor. In forty-five minutes a National Guard truck with a full-size military generator rumbled onto the battered ball field and parked next to the charred power pole. While we worked on recabling the generator, the Highsteppers got set up and the show forged ahead.

Everything was starting to feel like a crisis averted. One more band and we could put this lovely sweaty day behind us. It's pretty common in this land of humidity for late afternoon thunderheads to gather and drop some rain. Usually they build up slowly for a few hours and you have some time to assess the severity of the weather and get prepared. Not today. By the time Larry and co. were finishing their set, the sky went yellow gray, the wind barreled in and lightning starting to zing all around us. The promoter, having secured the box office, announced to the audience that we were done for the day and wished everybody better luck next time.

When the Blue Oyster Cult band members heard this, they jumped in their rental cars and busted out of the field of bad dreams. This was the tipping point for the local yahoos who had been grinding their teeth all day on white crosses and had polished off the last of the Jack Daniels. The next twenty minutes the stage was turned into a huge dumpster as every empty bottle that had been in front of the stage was thrown on the stage. Glass was exploding everywhere as my pals and I hunkered down behind the stage left P.A. speakers and waited for the ammo to run out.

When it seemed that the attack was winding down a half dozen REALLY angry patrons climbed up on the sound wing on the other side and rolled the entire system off and into the dirt. There were splintered cabinets, dislodged woofers, and flattened amp racks in a heap in front of the stage. It was at this time the skies opened up and a stinging monsoon of Tennessee rain and hail battered us all. The band crew and I made it to the semitrailer for shelter while the invading hordes called it a day and left. The rain lasted half an hour and then moved on as quickly as it had arrived. The sun came back out and coaxed the humidity back to unbearable. No promoter, no stage hands, no cops and half of my sound system laid shattered in the mud. We retrieved the rain soaked chunks of Bob's P.A. and picked out shards of broken glass from the band gear. The damage was substantial and we all took some comfort in knowing it would be a few days before we used this stuff for putting on another show.

The "big time" had been filled with surprises. I had been on the road for only one month and logged eight thousand miles driving in a van with six grown men. I saw my partner get stabbed and poured Gene Simmons' vomited stage blood out of the monitors. Lastly, I found myself on the receiving end of a bottle throwing, P.A. wrecking, tour stopping riot. The next day after our acrimonious encounter in Dixie, I landed at LAX and took a cab down Pacific Coast Highway to Hermosa Beach, the home of Tycobrahe Sound. I was the new kid and besides Bob and my two road partners, I had never met any of the other guys at my new place of employment. The taxi crested the last hill before town and I was welcomed to California by the sun setting into the Pacific and an ocean breeze on my face. Fellow road warriors greeted me and clamored for a blow by blow description of the chaos and destruction of the day before. Soon everyone was sharing their scariest memories of combat on the road and I felt accepted as a new member of a very small and unique fraternity. An hour later I was on the beach with a beer in my hand and a joint in my mouth. My youthful optimism had returned and any doubts I may have had about the touring life were washed away. In three days I would be rested, refreshed, and back on the road.

CHAPTER 6
CAMPING WITH PIRATES

Back on the road, I would go from the Blue Oyster Cult to Black Oak Arkansas. Based in the Ozark Hills of northern Arkansas, BOA played twin lead guitar, shit-kicking southern rock and roll boogie. Everybody had a grits and gravy nickname. There was Ricochet, Goober, Burly, Dirty, and Chickie Hawk. The managers were Butch and Sparky and the lead singer was Jim Dandy. Instead of the veiled mysticism of BOC, Black Oak was all about the party and playing anywhere, anytime. In 1973 they toured for ten months and made more money than any other act on the road that year including the Stones. They were relentless.

My first day with BOA, I had a private sit down with Butch the manager for a tour orientation talk in his motel room. His main concern was drug use, and specifically indulgence in cocaine. He made it clear Peruvian recreation would not be tolerated and would be cause for immediate dismissal. I assured him of my personal compliance. He shook my hand and welcomed me to the family. I was waiting to see if there were any other boundaries I needed to know about when he opened a suitcase on the bed next to me. It was full of neatly wrapped bars of high grade Lebanese hash. He pulled one out, broke it in two, and handed it to me without saying a word. Apparently the drug policy had special provisions. Butch gave me a fatherly pat on the back and sent me on my way with a smile. Clearly, this was a key element in pushing his herd of hippie hillbillies through three hundred shows a year without a mutiny.

Black Oak Arkansas at home

Cancellation of shows under any circumstance was unheard of. In my six months of service, we pulled out of only one show and that required an act of God. The gig was at a dirt racetrack in South Dakota and it had been raining for two weeks before we arrived. Our semi-truck was backed up to the deck and we rolled all of our gear onto the large plywood covered steel stage. As soon as the last case was pulled out, the scaffolding at the rear of the structure started sinking into the rain soaked earth underneath. The once level surface was now listing at a twenty degree angle and all of our road cases started rolling off on their own into the mud below. One third of our show made the plunge before we could stem the tide. At the same time, tornado sirens started blasting as the wind ripped the canvas skin from the roof. We sat in our van and hunkered down for two hours as the weather relentlessly assailed us. When it became clear there would be no way to put on a show, we began the task of fishing our gear out of the soup and loading it back into the truck.

Like my first tour, the seven-man crew and their bags traveled in a van with bench seats. Copious amounts of hashish helped maintain the sense of humor required for communal living in close quarters. For half a year we played six or seven shows a week and drove three to four hundred miles each night. A "day off" was for the 1000 mile drives. We got a shared room about once a week and truck stops were for upscale dining and shopping. To quote Chris Isaacs, it was camping with pirates.

From July to December we played over one hundred and fifty shows. Every night's set list was exactly the same as was Jim Dandy's between-song sermons. These were delivered with the passion of a country preacher and embraced an eclectic mix of sensibilities. His offerings were a mash up of mushroom influenced Southern Baptist parables sprinkled with Eastern spiritualism. The kids loved it.

Rick Perea was my new partner from Tycobrahe and had already been touring with Black Oak months before I got there. Rick was five or six years older than me and was a student of the "Bob Bogdanovich School of Indifference." His style was one hundred and eighty degrees opposite of my serious and earnest Midwest demeanor. I became his pet project as he endeavored to teach me how not to give a fuck about all the things that seemed important but weren't. He had a gift and I was fortunate to sit at the feet of the master. His first self appointed task was encouraging me to get rid of my denim cowboy hat.

"Raymond...that hat is terrible. I don't think you should wear it anymore."

I was caught off guard by this very specific critique of my fashion sense. This was coming from a man wearing a polyester shirt with a huge locomotive printed on it. I packed away my Midwest hippie helmet and never looked back.

* * *

Promoters would stack as many bands as they could get away with on the bill. Some of the acts supporting us that year were Foghat, The

Stampeders, Nazareth, Triumvirate, Leo Kottke, Wet Willie, Charlie Daniels, Robin Trower, and Montrose.

We always had at least two or three opening acts, and since Rick didn't care, I would mix their sound. The ongoing challenge in this setting was trying to get the audio balance right in a very short period of time. Everyday Little Dave and the Black Oak crew would assemble their huge backline of drums and amps. After a soundcheck, the remaining bands would build their setups in front of each other with the goal of having enough room left for the first band to stand on stage. Rick and I would mic up the first band and off we'd go. It was rock and roll party time. When band number one was done playing, we'd peel off their gear and throw the same microphones up on the next band. I would go back out front to the audio desk in time to start mixing band number two. The process was repeated until we ran out of bands and it was time for the headliners. This shotgun approach rarely resulted in audio excellence. Overall production goals favored quantity over quality. Bad sound was better than no sound. My new skill set focused on fast turn around times and keeping the bar low.

After resetting the stage for Black Oak, my final task was to prep the sound console for Chickie Hawk to mix his band. Originally the lead singer before Jim Dandy, he had been their one and only sound man since the beginning and was one sweetheart of a good old boy. It was two days before Christmas and the last show before the holidays. The next day would be the start of our first time off since July. I was sitting out front with Scottie Parsons, the band's forever lighting director, and starting my changeover of the sound desk in anticipation of the Black Oak sound man. Scottie was a true blue Memphis hipster and another extended Ozark family member. He was also the unofficial crew pharmacist and a trusted source for controlled substances, except the forbidden cocaine. Weed, speed and, mushrooms. Normal roadie stuff. Scottie also had some very nice LSD. Clean and mellow, his product provided a very manageable and pleasant cruise in low doses. Scottie felt he and I should get a head start on the holidays and split a hit. Except for load out, my work was done. There was no driving that night as we were all getting rooms. I accepted his glad tidings. Happy holidays. Happy trails.

We indulged and waited for the band. As I started to feel the warmth of our psychedelic supplements in my bones, I spotted Chickie Hawk's cowboy hat floating above the crowd coming in my direction. I watched it get closer and closer in slow motion until it stopped in front of me with it's tall lanky owner standing underneath. In his sweet, slow Ozark drawl, Chicken Hawk explains to me he wants to spend more time road managing the band and is looking for someone to take over his duties as sound man. He wants me to get the first chance at the position and thought tonight would be a good time to give it a shot. Chickie Hawk and his hat turned around and disappeared back into the crowd. As I took in this fresh bit of news with distracted amusement, the house lights went dark and the boys plugged in. Game on. I proceeded to mix the shit out of that show with lysergic precision. I was operating with no adult supervision and thoroughly enjoying it. Two hours went by like two minutes and I was just getting started. All too soon, the band was done and the house lights were back on.

It was apparent Scottie and I would need a couple of beers to focus on load out. I turned to climb off the mixing platform and in front of me stood the band's trio of managers, Butch, Sparky, and Chickie Hawk. I was face to face with the band's decision makers and was apprehensive about where this conversation was going to go. They were animated and excited. Their collective opinion was unanimous. I was told the band had never sounded better and they wanted me to be the new sound engineer when they toured again. Since I was still tripping my brains out, I decided to delay any discussions regarding employment or any other topics of a serious nature. I politely excused myself and returned to the task at hand. Securing beers and loading the truck were my immediate priorities. Our semi was packed and out of there in less than an hour and the six-month non-stop tour was over.

I spent the holidays at my parent's house back in Wichita. It took a week of Gloria's roast turkey, mashed potatoes, and fried chicken to start to feel normal again. In the seventies, being on the road for half a year was like being in outer space. You didn't see the news or read a paper. You were completely unaware of current events or the real world. All that mattered was setting up the gig, doing the gig, loading out the gig, and driving to the next one. It was a comforting sort of numbness once you surrendered to the routine.

Studies have shown that the young adult male human is drawn to lifestyle patterns that support the denial of the maturation process. Being on the road allows one to participate in a number of adolescence prolonging endeavors. No rent or bills to pay. No predictable small town obligations. Just a wishful concept of freedom fueled by too much fun. Even though I was beginning to embrace living in bizarro world, I had missed my family and music. After Christmas, I hung out with my old friends, John and Chuck, playing guitar and listening to my records. I hadn't touched an instrument in eight months and realized how much I had missed it. There was a lot to be said for familiar and normal, but after two weeks back in Wichita, I started to get the panicky feelings of being someplace where nothing ever changes. I recognized the symptoms. It was time to go.

> *"He wants his home and security*
> *He wants to live like a sailor at sea"*
> *Beautiful Loser*
> *Bob Seeger*

> *"Living on the road my friend was*
> *Gonna keep you free and clean*
> *And now you wear your skin like iron*
> *And your breath as hard as kerosene*

> *You weren't your mama's only boy*
> *But her favorite one it seems*
> *She began to cry when you said goodbye*
> *And sank into your dreams"*
> *Pancho and Lefty*
> Townes Van Zandt

CHAPTER 7
THE ELEMENTS OF
THE UNIVERSE

After Christmas, I slowly made my way back to California stopping in Colorado for a few weeks to recharge my hippie guitar playing batteries and see old friends. It made me happy but it didn't make me any money. When the Tycobrahe home office tracked me down in snow-packed Steamboat Springs, I was ready for another run. Earth, Wind and Fire was my next assignment. No disrespect to my two previous clients but these cats were serious and could play anything. They were smoking musicians, incredible singers, and were on the doorstep of worldwide success. Unfortunately, I was drafted to be their new monitor mixer and struggled, to say the least. I was christened "Ray Feedback" by the entire band. In my defense, I was issued a front of house board with two stereo outputs to satisfy the individual fold back needs of eight players and that was not a set up for success.

Having said that, I believe it is a poor craftsman who blames his tools and I was basically over my head. Learning the finer points of monitor mixing with a smaller band would have been a smarter way to develop my skills but that luxury was not an option. Meeting the monitor needs of a rock band demands the empathy of a therapist and the savvy of a hostage negotiator. I was more comfortable practicing my craft a hundred feet away at the front of house mixing console. The band and I soldiered through two long months of shows and, thankfully, my lack of chops did not derail their career. When the EW&F tour was over, I went back to Hermosa Beach and worked in the repair shop fixing P.A.'s while waiting for the next tour opportunity.

Two offers appeared at the same time. I had a choice of return-ing to the urban flames of Blue Oyster Cult or packing my belongings and moving to the Ozarks to live in the Black Oak family fort. At that time, the workaholic group owned the northern one-third of Arkansas and had built a village for the band, crew, managers, spouses, and children. Early proponents of self sufficient communal living, they had surrounded their entire compound with a ten-foot high wood fence. It was "F Troop" for hippies. I was leaning towards Black Oak since there was already an offer on the table to be their full time engineer. After my rocky ride at the monitor desk, I knew mixing out front was where I should be. As the new kid at the company, I also knew it would be a while before all the guys with seniority were going to let me near the cool bands. I was struggling to wrap my head around the reality of surrendering a year of my life doing another three hundred identical shows with the band who never stopped. I wasn't overjoyed with my options but it was looking like it was time for me to man up, shut up, and make some grown up money.

Out of nowhere, the fates magically presented me with a unique third choice. My touring spiritual advisor, Rick Perea, called me at the shop and asked if I was interested in driving the equipment truck for Fleetwood Mac. He said "Raymond, I think you should drive the truck for these guys." Ever since my first day with Black Oak, Rick had decided my name would be Raymond and not Ray. Rick's close friend, John Courage, was Fleetwood Mac's road manager and needed to find somebody soon. It was a five-week run across the states and they would pay me cash. In all my time working on the road, driving in some capacity was always part of the gig. This, of course, didn't take place until you had put in twelve hours putting on a show. The concept of only driving and not doing damage control for a shitty promoter wasn't a terrible thing. I would have hours of alone time with my guitar and make enough money to go hang out in Colorado for a while if there were no attractive tour offers. Heeding the advice of my esteemed mentor, I chose the fork in the road that would later prove to have life-long implications and repercussions.

★ ★ ★

The Aquarius Theatre in Hollywood on Sunset Blvd. was built in the 1930's as a swinging nightclub and dinner theatre. Originally named for it's owner, show biz mogul Earl Carroll, it would eventually become the Moulin Rouge nightclub and later hosted the TV shows "Queen for a Day" and "Hullabaloo". Sometime in the late sixties it was renamed the Aquarius in homage to the Los Angeles production of *Hair.* On this day in May of 1975 it would be the site of my first encounter with the retooled Fleetwood Mac. The band had just finished their first album with new members Lindsey Buckingham and Stevie Nicks and were rehearsing for a short tour across the states in theaters, auditoriums, and armories. They had spent the previous three months recording a great album but had never played in front of an audience together. This little run of shows would serve as a tune up for the real tour when the record was released in the summer.

The band had just finished their final rehearsal when I parked my Ryder rental truck by the back door. The crew was breaking down and the band was milling around. I only knew a couple of the guys there. Rick Perea and Mark Drale from Tycobrahe, and John Courage, my new boss. I was already settling into my new role as the random unknown truck driver and wasn't particularly motivated to get involved in the social fabric of a new bunch of strangers. Keeping to myself and observing the party from a distance was more in my comfort zone. John Courage, aka JC, pointed out the band members to me. Mick, at six-foot-six stood out, as he always does, in his tailored jeans and silk vest. He was involved with Curry Grant, the lighting director, in an animated discussion about the staging. Stevie and Christine were talking on a couch while John was sitting on the drum riser changing his bass strings. Lastly, I saw Lindsey showing sound man Richard Dashut a grocery bag of guitar parts that had once been his favorite Telecaster. It had been sent to a repairman for some new frets and was mysteriously returned in multiple pieces. The presence of Mick's two young daughters and wife filled the room with a civility and grown up family atmosphere not normally present at seventies rock band functions. Usually they were more like a boy's high school locker room or a demented frat house.

I always had a knack for loading trucks. Bob had taught me one of the tricks to getting respect from local stagehands was a firm command of the truck pack. Conversely, the quickest way to piss everyone off and lose your helpers is to be indecisive and a weenie about what road case is next to go in the truck. The ultimate sacrilege is spending an hour loading an entire forty-foot semi with a dozen east coast Teamsters only to get to the end and have boxes left over. Pity the fool who tries to convince these generous souls to unload your truck so you can try to figure out what went wrong and put it all back in a second time.

Curry Grant

It took hours to get the yellow Ryder rental truck loaded that first night. The twenty-six—foot box was the largest bobtail you could get before moving up to a semi truck, and tour manager John Courage was determined to not make that upgrade. Lighting, band gear, and a sound system all had to fit. Eventually it did after hours of loading, unloading and reloading. It was packed to the ceiling and all the way to the to the back door. It was so tight that I would need to stand on the brakes a couple of times before unloading to get the gear moved forward enough to roll up the door. Obviously overweight, the box was just a couple of inches above the rear tires. This was an ongoing issue throughout my trip as I received at least twenty tickets at weigh stations across the country. Different states had their own criteria for load limits. I was usually OK on the front axle but would have issues with the tonnage on the rear. If I was just a little over on my first weigh in, I would drive around to the rear of the weigh station, pull some guitar amps out of the back and stuff them in the cab with me. I would drive through a second time and wait for the results. If successful I would get off the scales, pull over, and return whatever I had packed in the cab back in the box and resume my drive.

A cabover is a specific truck design that has the cab sitting over the engine instead of behind it. The driver's compartment tilts forward to gain access to the motor for checking fluids and performing maintenance. It is also the easiest path to the device attached to the carburetor known as a governor. A governor is installed by the rental company and its sole purpose is to put a cap on how fast your truck can go. This was, of course, unacceptable and disabling the annoyance was my first order of business. The inside of my cab was bare bones. Ten speed Hi-Lo transmission, no a/c, no radio, no CB, and no radar detector. I brought my boom box, headphones, guitar, and a box of cassettes. A big bag of workingman's weed and a bottle of white crosses completed the luxury appointments that would be my creature comforts for the next five weeks.

FLEETWOOD MAC WARM UP TOUR
MAY 1975

15	EL PASO TEXAS	EL PASO CIVIC CENTER
16	AMARILLO TEXAS	CIVIC CENTER COLISEUM
17	ABILENE TEXAS	TAYLOR COUNTY EXPOSITION
18	DALLAS TEXAS	MEMORIAL AUDITORIUM
19	SAN ANTONIO TEXAS	MUNICIPAL AUDITORIUM
20	AUSTIN TEXAS	AUDITORIUM
21		
22	DETROIT MICHIGAN	MICHIGAN PALACE
23	AKRON OHIO	CIVIC CENTER
24	FT. WAYNE INDIANA	VETERAN'S MEMORIAL ARENA
25	SOUTH BEND INDIANA	MORRIS CIVIC AUDITORIUM
26		
27	OXFORD OHIO	MILLET AUDITORIUM
28		
29	DARBY PENNSYLVANIA	TOWER THEATER
30		
31	RICHMOND VIRGINIA	MOSQUE

JUNE 1975

01	WASHINGTON D.C.	CONSTITUTION HALL
02		
03	PITTSBURGH PENNSYLVANIA	STANLEY THEATER
04	TRENTON NEW JERSEY	WAR MEMORIAL HALL
05	BUFFALO NEW YORK	CENTURY THEATER
06	HEMPSTEAD LONG ISLAND	CALDRON THEATER
07	PASSAIC NEW JERSEY	CAPITOL THEATER
08	WATERBURY CONNECTICUT	PALACE THEATER

CHAPTER 8
NEVER SAY NEVER

The crew—two sound men, three band roadies, and two lighting guys—traveled in the "Executive", a rented motor home. The band traveled by commercial airlines. JC, the tour manager, Curry, the lighting director, and Richard, the sound mixer, would drive the band in rented station wagons if the trip was short enough.

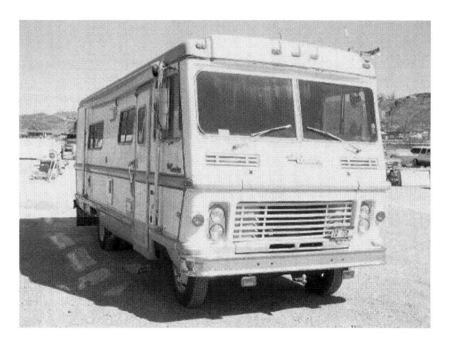

The Executive

Chris Nicks, Stevie's brother, came along as a band roadie to schlep Lindsey's guitars and amps. Lindsey had never toured with a helper before and was used to taking care of himself. This worked in Chris' favor as he didn't have a clue about guitars or amps. Chris did have substantial expertise in finding and acquiring high quality marijuana. This talent was of equal importance to Lindsey so any technical knowledge that Chris lacked was easily overlooked.

The first show was in El Paso in an old concrete convention center. I had spent the last year mixing in a hundred of these places and the mushy cavelike sound was always dreadful. I stayed for one song of the soundcheck and headed to my motel room to rest up for the next drive. Poor bastards, day one and it was already audio hell.

The next couple of weeks was a lot of driving with lots of miles between gigs. I wouldn't spend a lot of time at the shows because that was my rest time. Truthfully, I had grown weary of hearing a bunch of random bands boogie the night away. I would usually stay after we unloaded the truck in the morning and help Chris Nicks plug in Lindsey's gear in exchange for an afternoon nap reefer. It was nice having quiet time alone instead of wrestling another gig into audio submission.

Chris would occasionally ride with me and help drive on long runs. On one of those trips the cable for the accelerator broke from the pedal. We were in the middle of nowhere at four in the morning and dead in the water. Chris spent the last hundred miles of the drive on the floor sitting between my legs holding the accelerator cable with a pair of vice grips. He would have to pull it in to give it the gas and then release it every time I shifted. The proximity of his face to my crotch for ninety minutes established a new and lasting bond between us.

The last time Mr. Nicks rode with me was near the end of the tour when we were in the Northeast heading to NYC. We had overnight to get from Buffalo to Long Island. I had been to the city a couple of times before but never as the driver. I had one road atlas and it lacked clarity in regards to the roads in and out of town. To avoid the highways banning trucks we ended up going through the Holland Tunnel three times. Each pass through took longer and longer as we struggled with rush hour. After the third time around we found ourselves at the same ramp with the same two choices. Back to the Holland Tunnel or on to the "No Trucks Allowed" Thruway straight to Hempstead. We were out of options. Our map sucked and there were no gas stations to ask for help.

Exhausted and late for load in I made the executive decision to take the forbidden road. What was the worst that could happen? Get a ticket? I already had a glove box full of them. It would be the price of doing business as far as I was concerned. I was almost at freeway speed when we saw the reason why this route was for passenger cars only. Directly in front of us stood an aging brick overpass built in an era that did not anticipate the overhead clearance required for modern day trucking. I downshifted hard and stood on the brakes aiming for the high spot in the center of the arched span. Cars were passing me on both sides as I stayed in the middle of the three lanes and stopped feet short of the ancient bridge. Chris leaned halfway out of his window and clung to the side mirror as he eyeballed our margin. I inched towards the concrete lip above us until I heard Chris yell. "We're good: let's hit it!" There were seven or eight more of these bridges in the next ten miles and we navigated each one the same way until we got to the toll booths. There were four booths and all the attendants came out to give me a hard time. I pulled out my Kansas drivers license and gave them my best "I'm not from around here." No citations were issued and we were at the gig in thirty minutes.

I slept most of the day and decided to go to the venue early and catch the end of the band's set. I walked out to the mixing desk about halfway through the show. I was stunned. What I heard was a completely different band than the one I heard in El Paso. Every song. Every instrument. Every vocal. Three great singers that switched off as background singers behind whoever was taking the lead. A sturdy seasoned English blues band rhythm section. Two beautiful and talented women. A powerful and unique guitarist. The simplicity of the instrumentation tamed the echo-soaked venue. There were no weaknesses. The five musicians on stage were all completely different and equally compelling. It was a good night and the crowd was going nuts. I wanted to see more.

The next night I made sure to be there for the whole show and was even more impressed. The night before wasn't a fluke. The three songwriters delivered a diversity of material that was deep and varied. I stayed for the whole show. These guys were really, really cool in so many ways and I was getting sucked in. I couldn't wait until the next show and was blown away that it was even better than the first two. All the parts and pieces hung effortlessly together and it felt like it had always been that way.

The last few days had been so unexpected and compelling. I had been trained as a soldier in the jungles of arena rock and was skilled in helping promoters get the most out of whatever they put on a stage. In my tool belt was a boat load of new audio skills acquired at the expense of any passion for the music. Destiny was in full effect and it was futile to question it. At the end of the last show of the tour, I found JC the tour manager. I told him I thought his band was doing everything right and I would be very interested in staying on as a part of the crew. He asked me what I had in mind and I suggested Chris Nicks and I trade jobs.

"Let me handle the band gear and give Chris the keys to the truck."

I hadn't discussed this with Chris yet but I doubted there would be any opposition. As far as my mixing future, Richard Dashut was doing a great job and the band was already committed to him. It didn't matter. I wanted the opportunity to bring something to this party. Just a month earlier, I was questioning whether I should continue helping other bands sound better when I could be playing my own music. This band was worthy of my support. My hopefully someday budding music career would have to wait.

After talking with the band, JC offered me the position of roadie third class. The first person I talked to after Courage was a relieved Chris Nicks. He said he was ready to move on to something more suited to his talents and happily accepted the player swap.

The tour was now completed and it was time to take everything back to California. Mick's roadie, Mike Miller, said he would help me drive if we could stop in his hometown, Kansas City. We made good time and rolled into town in two days. Mike drove us into the city and over to Superior Sound, the shop owned by my good friends Jim and Brock. It sat on the top of a hill that sloped all the way down to the city center. My buddy parked the truck just above the storefront and we made our way into the building to surprise my friends. We hung out for awhile and made plans for dinner. It was five in the afternoon and the busy street was filled with going home traffic. We walked out the front door of the shop and turned left to go back to the truck. Instead of seeing our trusted conveyance, we stared at a twenty-six-foot empty space. This was the most terrifying feeling I have ever had in my life. We stood speechless at the vacant curb. An entire tour of equipment had vanished. I looked to my right towards the business district. It was forty blocks downhill to downtown Kansas City. I was feeling every facet of disbelief, denial, and sick that I had ever known. This can't be happening.

WHERE THE FUCK IS MY TRUCK???!!!!!

And then…about twenty feet downhill on a residential street across from us sat a twenty-six-foot bright yellow Ryder truck. It was parked perfectly at the curb between the driveways of two houses right behind a '56 Chevy. Mike and I sprinted through the four lanes of traffic dodging cars in both directions. We got to the cabover and slowly approached the front of the vehicle. I felt for my keys and started to panic until I realized Mike still had them. We peeked warily inside the windows from each side not knowing if we were in the middle of a truck jacking. The cab was still locked and empty. The front bumper was tight against the back bumper of the Chevy. The old Bel Air was unharmed.

There were no scratches, dents or any other signs of impact. I took the keys from Mike, got in and did a quick inventory. The parking brake was still on and the transmission was in first gear. I rolled down my window and looked back across the street at my friends' store and the bobtail truck-sized stretch of empty curb in front. I got back out and circled the rock and roll rental to assess damages and look for clues. Everything looked fine and seemed untouched. The tires on the passenger side were wedged tight against the curb and there was fresh rubber on the concrete edge all the way back to the first driveway. I looked all around expecting someone to appear with the authorities in tow. If anybody saw what happened they were keeping it to themselves.

Since no one was stepping up to offer an eyewitness account, we pieced together the only conclusion that made any sense. It would seem that our truck took itself for a little solo drive. Mike confessed to me that he might not have turned the front wheels into the curb when we parked. I made a mental note to never let him behind the wheel again. Not only did he not set the wheels safely, he left them slightly turned towards the street. That enabled the overweight box on wheels to make a long slow left turn on its own and roll in first gear across all four lanes of rush hour traffic untouched. The marginally functioning parking brake kept the momentum contained until it reached the curb of the cross street. The tires then apparently wedged themselves into the cement lip for forty feet until it gently stopped itself on the rear bumper of the parked Chevy. There was no other explanation.

No harm no foul. A force larger than the both of us had intervened and left us to live another day without inflicting human carnage or getting arrested. I got behind the wheel and we silently left the scene of the nearly committed crime. I dropped Mike off at his house and headed out to dinner with my friends. The next day I drove by myself down to Wichita for a day with the folks and then took everything back to L.A. I spent many of the following weeks reflecting on the negative impact this incident could have had on my future in the music business, not to mention prison time.

CHAPTER 9
TAKE COURAGE

One of the things I learned in my year touring with Tycobrahe Sound as an audio engineer was the pecking order of power at a typical rock show. It was a crazy time when the audience cared more about how the bands sounded than how bright the lights were. The P.A. company was closer to the top of the food chain. There were no stage managers so it was on us to steer the flow of the support bands. The headliner was paying for the sound system and was the pack leader. That left a limited number of trees for the remaining groups to piss on.

Helping others to coexist peacefully was all part of a day at the office but there were occasional unfortunate misunderstandings. One of the tools we had in resolving stage conflicts was the power to turn off the P.A. system until clearer heads prevailed. It never failed to help cut through the bullshit. Every band on the bill had it's own unique organizational footprint and personality. Many were self sufficient, on top of their game and willing to behave rationally. Others were like rugby scrums with ex-cons.

Most acts usually had two guys who covered everything their band needed to get them from town to town and up on stage no matter what. The English roadies were extra passionate about their turf and articles of entitlement. Clearly cooler than their Yankee counterparts, they usually dressed better and had hipper haircuts. They were also like little biker gangs without motorcycles. Their dedication to their band had a passion that is likely traced to WWII England and the lean years of nation rebuilding following the war. For the majority of kids born in wartime England, growing up was filled with getting by on very little and having no fear of fighting for what you did have. An abundance of British blues bands in the sixties were populated with hungry young men looking for something sunny in the rainy grey UK. Bands were competitive and often overbooked by club owners. Ensuring a space on stage was the first step to getting paid and the band's crew were the first responders. The basic road skills of driving and schlepping gear were coupled with the fearless determination of a mama bear protecting her cubs. A pirate spirit of "don't fuck with us" was encouraged and embraced by bands and management.

In spite of an arrogance inspired by five hundred years of British Empire world dominance, I found these tea sipping, whiskey guzzling Anglos absolutely enjoyable to hang with. They told you exactly how they felt and expected the same in return. Their dry humor and posh accent could make the invitation to "go fuck yourself" sound charming and generous. Besides a fierce loyalty to their bands, there was a shared awareness that this rock and roll stuff was neither sacred or precious. One thing we all agreed on was that what ever it was we were doing was better than "working".

★ ★ ★

For the most part I directed my energies toward the hardware side of things and steered away from the antics of those darn humans. I loved mixing and making P.A.'s work. I loved bands and music. I was undecided about musicians but drawn to their chaos. My nerdy penchant for organizing and fixing things had found a home in a noisy twisted tribe dedicated to making a mess and breaking stuff. Working for the sound company filled me with the illusion that I was above the dysfunction and I could never see myself in the less structured world of traveling with a band.

John Courage, also known as JC or "The Colonel" was the man responsible for bringing me into the Fleetwood Mac family and changing my perspective about being a band roadie. JC had worked for

Christine's band Chicken Shack and blues band Savoy Brown before joining Fleetwood Mac as road manager, sound man, and roadie in 1972. He was the embodiment of all things British and seventies abandon. When necessary, he could be arrogant, officious, and unyielding. However, these were the tools of his trade and not a reflection of the inner man. Taking a rock band around the world in those days was not a glamorous task. Pre-fame rockers were not generally embraced outside of their milieu. JC had little patience for opportunists and agents of bullshit. He demanded and received respect for his traveling family.

In JC's early days with the band touring the States, he devised a plan to get the airlines to assist with transporting the band gear around the country. Courage would go to the airport early in the morning with the band's tickets and check in 25 or 30 cases of guitars, amps and drums as excess baggage and then leave the tickets with the agent to hold for the group when they arrived later. He then flew to the next town, got a rental truck and waited for the group and their "bags". If he found the right guy to talk to, he would even drive straight onto the tarmac and get the bag handlers to load road cases straight into his truck. No one thought twice about security and everybody was always receptive to making a little extra cash. Simpler times.

Mick, John, and Christine loved and trusted him. They knew he always had their backs in spite of occasional lapses of public decorum. Ninety percent of their day was spent at airports, restaurants, and hotels at the mercy of uninspired civilians. The remaining ten percent was onstage at the mercy of promoters, unions, and the headline bands. Creating a controlled and consistent performing environment for the players was JC's sole mission and he was unswerving in his struggle to make things right for his fellow countrymen. Mr. Courage was a true believer in these principles and way of life. His critics may take issue with his style but they never walked in his shoes. My perception of band roadie was elevated when I got to know this fucking crazy man and his warm ways.

John Courage

Fleetwood Mac was originally formed in 1967. In two years, England's premier blues band became the top group in the United Kingdom over the Beatles and Stones. One year later in 1970 the band's leader, guitarist Peter Green, shocked the music world and the rest of his band when he announced his retirement. The band continued recording and touring with Christine McVie and various combinations of guitar players. When the band took an unplanned break in 1973, long time manager Clifford Davis decided to claim ownership of the band name for himself.

Casting scruples and good manners aside, he assembled a pack of blues players, christened them "Fleetwood Mac" and sent them off on tour. As an employee of Clifford Davis, JC was coerced into working the tour. He didn't realize the extent of the bait and switch until the first show and was instrumental in finding Mick and exposing the scam.

The real Fleetwood Mac picked up on the ruse and initiated litigation to determine legally whose band it was. Drummer Fleetwood and bassist McVie seemed to to have the upper hand in this decision as the band was named after them. Until the courts made a ruling, however, the band's royalties from their previous albums as Fleetwood Mac would be held by their record company Warner Bros. The band— Mick, John, Christine and guitarist Bob Welch along with JC—stayed in LA and recorded a new album while their lawsuit crawled through the court system.

At the end of 1974, Bob Welch left to pursue a solo career. Once again, FM was without a guitar player as well as a manager. Throughout the band's history of exits and reincarnations, Mick had always taken on the task of finding the next guitarist. A self taught musician, Fleetwood was in no way properly schooled in his vocation. Mick's gift as a drummer is his ability to immerse himself in the emotion of his front man/woman and let his playing be guided by the feel. When a guitar player/singer/ songwriter left the fold, the powerhouse percussionist was beyond unemployed—he was adrift without a muse. Any leanings towards being the leader or manager were based solely on his survival instincts as a drummer in a band. His accidental discovery of Stevie and Lindsey while looking at recording studios was the kind of cosmic gift that has always drifted around the Fleetwood Mac universe and Mick was perfectly poised to channel it their direction.

JC, Christine & Stevie

I knew nothing about this truth is stranger than fiction rock legacy when I was hired by the "Colonel" to drive the band's truck on their first tour. For me, it was an opportunity to make some cash while I weighed my future as a touring sound man. In a few short weeks I went from casual indifference about a random rock band to born again believer in the unlimited possibilities of rock and roll. JC had earned his place with the band through years of loyal service during strange and lean times. His devotion to their success and music was pure and undying. He was my mentor, tormentor, role model, and loyal friend. I approached handling the band's gear with the knowledge and ear of a sound engineer and JC showed me how to apply those skills Fleetwood Mac style. I was now a band roadie but a John Courage trained Ray Lindsey band roadie. Through JC I came to understand that this band's power as a whole was greater than the sum of it's parts and our contribution was the stewardship of that complex and unpredictable chemistry. It was meant to be. ... Get some rest, John. I'll drive for a while.

Me and "the Colonel" Germany 1980

JULY 1975
FLEETWOOD MAC *FLEETWOOD MAC* TOUR

04	HONOLULU HAWAII	DIAMOND HEAD CRATER
05		
06	ANCHORAGE ALASKA	

AUGUST 1975

01	SAN BERNARDINO CALIFORNIA	SWING AUDITORIUM
02		
03	OAKLAND CALIFORNIA	OAKLAND COLISEUM
04	LOS ANGELES CALIFORNIA	
05		
06		
07	VANCOUVER BRITISH COLUMBIA	P.N.E. GARDENS
08	SEATTLE WASHINGTON	PARAMOUNT THEATER
09	PORTLAND OREGON	PARAMOUNT THEATER
10	MISSOULA MONTANA	FIELD HOUSE UNIVERSITY OF MONTANA
11	LETHBRIDGE ALBERTA CANADA	MUNICIPAL AUDITORIUM
12	EDMONTON ALBERTA CANADA	JUBILEE AUDITORIUM
13	CALGARY ALBERTA CANADA	JUBILEE AUDITORIUM
14		
15	MILWAUKEE WISCONSIN	ARENA
16	MINNEAPOLIS MINNESOTA	METROPOLITAN SPORTS ARENA
17	KANSAS CITY MISSOURI	MEMORIAL HALL
18	ST. LOUIS MISSOURI	CONCERT SOUTH CLUB
19	ST. LOUIS MISSOURI	CONCERT SOUTH CLUB
20	WICHITA KANSAS	CENTURY II THEATER
21		
22	ALBUQUERQUE NEW MEXICO	CIVIC AUDITORIUM

23 FLAGSTAFF ARIZONA   NORTH ARIZONA
                                UNIVERSITY
24 PHOENIX ARIZONA   CELEBRITY THEATER
25
26
27
28
29 MODESTO CALIFORNIA   ICE ARENA
30 ANAHEIM CALIFORNIA   ANAHEIM STADIUM
31 SAN DIEGO   BALBOA STADIUM

                    SEPTEMBER 1975
01 FRESNO CALIFORNIA   MADERA SPEEDWAY
02
03
04
05
06
07
08
09
10
11 SALT LAKE CITY UTAH   TERRACE BALLROOM
12 DENVER COLORADO   MCNICHOLS ARENA
13 GRAND JUNCTION COLORADO   MESA JUNIOR COLLEGE
14 CASPER WYOMING   FAIRGROUNDS
15
16 LINCOLN NEBRASKA   PERSHING AUDITORIUM
17 MADISON WISCONSIN   DANE COUNTY
                                COLISEUM
18 CHICAGO ILLINOIS   AUDITORIUM THEATER
19 CARBONDALE ILLINOIS   SOUTHERN ILLINOIS
                                UNIVERSITY
20 WEST LAFAYETTE INDIANA   PERDUE UNIVERSITY
                                HALL OF MUSIC

21	CINCINNATI OHIO	EDGEWATER RACEWAY PARK
22		
23	LACROSSE WISCONSIN	MARY E. SAWYER AUDITORIUM
24	DAVENPORT IOWA	THE ORPHEUM
25	NORMAL ILLINOIS	UNIVERSITY AUDITORIUM
26	CLEVELAND OHIO	KENT STATE UNIVERSITY BALLROOM
27	DETROIT MICHIGAN	MICHIGAN THEATER
28	INDIANAPOLIS INDIANA	STADIUM

OCTOBER 1975

03	HAMPTON ROADS VIRGINIA	HAMPTON COLISEUM
04	RICHMOND VIRGINIA	RICHMOND COLISEUM
05	LANDOVER MARYLAND	CAPITAL CENTRE
06		
07		
08	ROCHESTER NEW YORK	WAR MEMORIAL AUDITORIUM
09	BUFFALO NEW YORK	CENTURY THEATER
10	UNIONDALE LONG ISLAND	NASSAU COLISEUM
11	PHILADELPHIA PENNSYLVANIA	THE SPECTRUM
12	JOHNSTON PENNSYLVANIA	UNIVERSITY OF PENNSYLVANIA
13		
14	SYRACUSE NEW YORK	LOEW'S THEATER
15	PITTSBURGH PENNSYLVANIA	CIVIC ARENA
16	ERIE PENNSYLVANIA	ERIE COUNTY FIELD HOUSE
17	PASSAIC THEATER	CAPITOL THEATER
18	BOSTON MASSACHUSETTS	BOSTON GARDENS
19	ALBANY NEW YORK	PALACE THEATER
20	NEW HAVEN CONNECTICUT	NEW HAVEN COLISEUM

21 UNION NEW JERSEY
22
23
24 HAMILTON NEW YORK   COLGATE UNIVERSITY
25 STORRS CONNECTICUT   UNIVERSITY OF
                                        CONNECTICUT
26 NEW YORK NEW YORK   BEACON THEATER 2
                                        SHOWS
27
28
29
30

NOVEMBER 1975

12 BIRMINGHAM ALABAMA   MUNICIPAL
                                        AUDITORIUM
13 KNOXVILLE TENNESSEE   COLISEUM
14 ATLANTA GEORGIA   FOX THEATER
15 CHARLESTON WEST VIRGINIA   MUNICIPAL
                                        AUDITORIUM
16 GREENSBORO NORTH CAROLINA   PIEDMONT SPORTS
                                        ARENA
17
18 CHAPEL HILL NORTH CAROLINA   CARMICHAEL
                                        AUDITORIUM
19 WILSON NORTH CAROLINA   ATLANTIC CHRISTIAN
                                        COLLEGE
20 WINSTON SALEM NORTH CAROLINA   WAKE FOREST
                                        UNIVERSITY
21 MORGANTOWN WEST VIRGINIA   UNIVERSITY OF
                                        WEST VIRGINIA
22 HARRISONBURG VIRGINIA   MADISON COLLEGE
                                        GYM
23 CHARLOTTESVILLE VIRGINIA   UNIVERSITY OF
                                        VIRGINIA

24 - 30	HOMESTEAD FLORIDA
	REHEARSAL HOUSE

DECEMBER 1975

02	RAY LINDSEY 21ST BIRTHDAY!!!	
03	HOUSTON TEXAS	HOUSTON MUSIC HALL
04	DALLAS TEXAS	
05	AUSTIN TEXAS	
06	NEW ORLEANS LOUISIANA	THE WAREHOUSE
07		
08		
09	LAS CRUCES NEW MEXICO	NEW MEXICO STATE UNIVERSITY
10	TUCSON ARIZONA	TUCSON CONVENTION CENTER
11	DENVER COLORADO	DENVER CONVENTION CENTER
12	PHOENIX ARIZONA	PHOENIX CIVIC PLAZA
13	FRESNO CALIFORNIA	
14		
15		
16	SANTA BARBARA CALIFORNIA	UNIVERSITY OF CALIFORNIA
17		
18	BAKERSFIELD CALIFORNIA	BAKERSFIELD CIVIC AUDITORIUM
19	LOS ANGELES CALIFORNIA	THE FORUM
20	SAN DIEGO CALIFORNIA	SPORTS ARENA

CHAPTER 10
VOLCANOES AND GLACIERS

Diamond Head on the island of Oahu is the state of Hawaii's most recognizable landmark. It came by this name when British sailors in the late 1700's mistakenly thought the calcite crystals sparkling in the crater's lava rock were actually diamonds. Created five hundred thousand years ago by a single, massive eruption, the extinct volcano is capped by a broad, saucer-shaped crater. It's grassy three hundred and fifty acre interior, Diamond Head crater, is accessed solely through the two hundred and twenty-five-foot Kahala Tunnel. Once the home of an Army fort and a battery of cannons, it was also known as the site of a decade-long series of music happenings known as the Crater Festivals. Beginning on New Years Day in 1969, the all-day, sometimes weekend-long festivals were the pride of the island's counter culture. Crowds of twenty thousand locals filled the grounds with Age of Aquarius vibes and impressive quantities of pakalolo.

On July 4, 1975, I worked my first show as a roadie with Fleetwood Mac at that summer's Crater Celebration. On the bill supporting us was Canned Heat, Graham Central Station, Flo & Eddie, Lydia Pense & Cold Blood, and a handful of local musicians. This was the next to the last show I worked that was an old-fashioned total hippie free-for-all. There was no real "backstage". The crowd melted into the performance area and everything ran on island time. The audience was on their best behavior and all was chill. Canned Heat finished their set and I helped my new crew mates set up the Mac backline for my very first time. I was basking in the bohemian glory of my new station in life when a plume of black smoke began rising from the back of the crowd. In five minutes the sweet tropical trade winds whipped up a full-on brush fire by the back wall of the crater.

We watched from the stage as the crowd pulled back from the quickly growing flames. With the unlit tunnel as the only egress, the idyllic love fest had the potential to get ugly real quick. Our first course of action was to pack up our gear in case we had to shelter in place. JC and John McVie jumped in with the crew and we loaded our rental truck. As the last road case went in and I rolled down the door, we could hear a wailing siren in the distance. Conventional wisdom would suggest that the singular exit would be full of panicking escapees and any incoming fire fighting traffic would be shut down. This would absolutely be the case on the mainland, but on the islands, things moved in a different way. The tunnel stayed wide open and in a few minutes, an old pumper truck rumbled into the crater. The crowd parted and a straight path to the fire magically opened. As quickly as they appeared, the flames were gone and serenity returned to the masses.

Instead of a crazed mob clawing for survival there was an unfazed tribe of blissful Oahu hippies patiently waiting for the headline band to play. In the wake of this unexpected reprieve, we headed back to the stage and forged ahead with the show. The sun was disappearing into the ocean as we unloaded our truck for the second time and reset all the band gear. With no sound check and darkness falling, the band eased into an extended slinky intro to *Station Man.* A full moon rose over the back of the stage and filled the crater with a soft glow. Peace and love was in full effect as the band played in the sweet Hawaiian night.

My second show with the band was a one hundred and eighty-degree turnaround from the first. Thanks to an Aloha Airlines package that promoted a stop in Alaska after visiting Honolulu, we took an offer to play Anchorage after the Hawaii show. Any gig with the promise of cash for the band was embraced at this time. The previous year, in 1974, construction began on the Trans-Alaska Pipeline System, one of the world's largest petroleum conduits. Eight hundred miles of forty-eight-inch pipe were built to move crude oil from Prudhoe Bay to Valdez, Alaska where it was pumped onto gigantic ocean going tankers headed for the lower forty-eight. The project attracted tens of thousands of workers to the state, creating a boomtown atmosphere in Valdez, Fairbanks, and Anchorage. It was the 1970's version of the "Wild West."

Crews typically were out in the expansive Alaskan wilderness for a week or two at a time before returning to town for a few days of R & R, blowing all the excess cash they were making. Bars were open twenty-four hours a day and the once sleepy little Arctic towns were taken over by raging posses of pipeline cowboys.

Our five-hour flight took us from cosmic island serenity to fear and loathing on the tundra. There hadn't been a lot of music here besides the local bar bands and our arrival was the talk of the town. We got our gear off the plane and set out for the chosen venue. We arrived at an oversized steel quonset hut with a dirt floor and a homemade plywood stage that leaned to one side. The promoter's P.A. was a melange of six different little crappy systems all strung together with table lamp wire and Xmas tree extension cords. The monitors were three different home stereos. It was unbelievable. If we had been closer to standard civilization and a legitimate promoter, we would have demanded audio upgrades or pulled the plug on the show. However, there was nothing standard or legitimate about the 24/7 nonstop party that had embraced us as the guests of honor.

The room was packed to its corrugated roof and the natives were already restless. It was another rock show free-for-all with no backstage, no dressing rooms, and no security. The band assessed the few options left to them and chose to catch up to the locals and started drinking. We threw the band gear up on the listing deck and worked on getting rid of the loudest buzzes in the sound system. We couldn't lift many grounds without creating deadly voltage between the microphones and the band's instruments so we kept the buzzes.

Once the band attained proper blood alcohol levels they took to the stage. Thunderous applause greeted them and they shuffled some blues for awhile. This was cool until they started their first song with vocals and immediately smoked the faux monitor system. After a couple of attempts at trying to harmonize without hearing themselves, the set meandered back to various liquor fueled blues jams highlighted by numerous keyboard and guitar solos. There was possibly a bass solo as well. With no singing on the menu, Stevie was reduced to an entire set of tambourine and twirl. This forgettable night of liquid looseness proved to be the perfect soundtrack for our baked Alaskans. We ended the show with all the grace and dignity the room would allow. A quick load out and short drive later, we arrived at the only lodgings in town that could accommodate our entourage. Waiting for us there was an informal and uninvited afterparty consisting of most of the people who were at the gig. With more loathing but less fear, the never-ending happy hour searched all night in vain for last call. It was two a.m. but the Arctic summer sun made it look like six p.m. Fortunately, all our rooms had curtains as thick as carpeting to ensure an around the clock Elvis darkness. The day ended sometime the next morning as we finally sought refuge in our blacked out caves.

We had successfully adapted to our surroundings and gained the respect of a town filled with unhinged gin-soaked wackos. It was time to move on. The next day a few of us took a boat to Portage Glacier. Ten stories high and miles long, the gigantic ice cube at the end of a picturesque lake helped restore our perspective. It wasn't just the bar tabs that were huge in the forty-ninth state. Cleansed and refreshed, we returned to the airport. We loaded our guitars and amps into the cargo hold of an Aloha Airlines 737 and boarded the plane for our flight back home. Ironically, LA seemed like a safe and quiet destination.

CHAPTER 11
FLATLAND FOLLIES

My Fleetwood Mac band crew mates were Mike Miller and Ron "Rhyno" Penny. Both hailed from Kansas City and together we were the Flatland Follies. Rhyno and myself looked after the instrument and electronic side of the gear and Mike's job was the handling of the drums. Normally drum roadie was a pretty straight-ahead gig, but the owner of these drums was Mick Fleetwood and that's where normal and straight-ahead came to a screeching halt. Mick was not quite the madman as Keith Moon but was cut from the same expensive cloth. His insanity was not of a legal nature but was rooted in a caveman approach to music and living that embraced lunacy while appearing to walk through life as a proper English gentleman. His dedication to this lifestyle was entertaining and endearing. It also sucked the life out of anyone in the vicinity who was charged with accomplishing tasks involving order and discipline.

For these reasons, Mick has always required the largest team of support personnel, and in the early days of the original small machine, he was the only band member to have his own dedicated roadie. In the movie classic *Spinal Tap,* the fictitious band had a legacy of losing and replacing multiple drummers throughout their bumpy career. Fleetwood Mac had a similar reputation except it was the drummer's roadies that spun through the revolving door.

In Mick's defense, he was neither malicious or mean-spirited—he just had a lot going on. Most of the guys that came and went usually made the same common mistake. They underestimated the mystical power vortex that inhabited and ruled the world of Mick. He was a charming and knowing purveyor of chaos and bedlam. It was essential for the uninitiated to respect the beast or risk being devoured by it. For the most part, Mick's approach to life was all in good fun and a product of the coping mechanisms that develop after years of touring. I personally feel that exposure to the nightly explosions of drums and cymbals so close to one's head also contribute to a certain unpredictability. Initially, I too was drawn to his seductive looniness but quickly recognized that long-term employment would require at least an arm's length distance from the core of the reactor. My plan for survival was to keep myself immersed in speakers and wires and not be directly involved with drum kits or drummers. This tactic didn't offer total immunity but was useful in maintaining a defensible space.

Ron "Rhyno" Penny

Rhyno and I left Mike to his own fate while we wrangled the pieces of band gear called the backline. McVie's bass amps were either side of Mick's drum riser with Lindsey's equipment to his left and Christine's speakers and organ Leslies to his right. There were guitar extensions on Chris' side and keyboard speakers on Lindsey's side.

Both rows of boxes had the outside cabinets tilted towards Mick so he could be bombarded with the full volume of the band. The fortress of amps, speakers and drum riser covered almost forty feet. This was the old school approach to filling the stage with sound. Monitors were used primarily for vocals in the early days and the rest of the band gear did the heavy lifting.

Rhyno was four years my senior and far more outgoing in disposition. He was our ringleader, crew spokesman, and the perfect opposite to me. It wasn't exactly good cop, bad cop-more like loud cop quiet cop. I stayed with what I knew—loading the truck, fixing blown-up amplifiers, and making buzzes go away. The two of us covered a lot of ground.

ICA, Intercontinental Absurdities, was Frank Zappa's production company. Under it's umbrella was Frank's record and film companies and all of his touring support. He was the first outside act to buy his own Tycobrahe P.A. and he owned his own semi-truck to transport the show in. His company also operated it's own tour bus for Frank and his band to travel in while touring. Country bands had been traveling in coaches for years but the business of rock was just beginning to catch on to the convenience of having your own rolling bedroom. Zappa's custom bus had four "staterooms" with bunk beds and lounges fore and aft. Standard fare on the inside, but less so on the outside. Originally an authentic Greyhound bus, the company logo on the sides had been reworked Zappa style. Using the same familiar font and lettering, the name "Greyhound" was replaced with "Phydeaux" (pronounced Fido) and the sleek athletic dog in full stride ahead of the company name was now a limping one-eyed survivor of some unknown mishap.

Phydeaux

When Frank's band wasn't touring, ICA leased his bus out and our crew was treated to this stunning upgrade in roadie aesthetics. We already had our own semi-truck and driver, the esteemed Gilbert Lopez, and now we had eliminated the ubiquitous eight-passenger bench seat van. Thanks to tour manager John Courage and the still cash-strapped band, we would never again have to drive ourselves all night after working all day at the show. In addition, JC also demanded from every promoter that the crew was to be furnished with a hot meal for dinner. Accompanying that meal would be real, not paper, plates and proper non-plastic cutlery. Whether these gestures were a product of British good manners or just the wisdom of experience, they were a big deal.

In the fall of 1975, Fleetwood Mac was not yet a household name. Their core fans kept the home fires burning but the group's recent personnel changes and the taint of their old manager's fake band had put a dent in the band's identity. They reclaimed their stature with their newly discovered onstage chemistry. Mick, John, and Christine's years of experience playing together provided a launching pad for the already accomplished Lindsey and Stevie. The guitarist's confidence, power, and style grew every show while Stevie's stage persona crystallized and took flight. The band's new audiences were being treated to the first glimpse of what the future was bringing and the energy was snowballing.

By October, every show was a powerhouse and our small machine was rampaging through the countryside, taking one town after another. Our crew of eight lived and breathed as one. We felt like an out of nowhere underdog college basketball team on a winning streak. March Madness was in sight and we were destined for the finals.

★ ★ ★

Loggins and Messina were a successful duo from the early seventies and their rock didn't get any smoother. Among their best known songs are *Danny's Song, House At Pooh Corner,* and *Your Mama Don't Dance.* Jim Messina, formerly of Poco and Buffalo Springfield, was working for Columbia Records as a producer in 1970 when he met Kenny Loggins, a singer/ songwriter and guitarist. The two were an effective writing and recording team and sold over sixteen million records during their peak years. The emerging college/FM radio market embraced the easy listening duo and for four years they raked it in selling out shows everywhere. By the end of 1975 the shine was off the apple and their arena-sized audiences were starting to thin out. The halcyon days of guaranteed sell outs were fading away. Promoters would supplement anemic ticket sales by adding strong opening acts to co-bill and Fleetwood Mac was the perfect up-and-coming crowd pleaser needed to help fill the seats.

L&M had been big dogs for a few years and were quite comfortable with their place in the world. Jim was a bit of a control freak and made it clear to everybody, including Kenny and the band, who was in charge. During sound checks before he arrived, the band of shit-hot players would brazenly jam until their leader showed up. Jim didn't want his guys playing anything but his music and he was opposed to this display of abandon. If the band didn't get a heads up from a roadie when the boss man was close, they would receive a tongue lashing and reprimand from their band leader.

Our first show opening for Loggins and Messina was October 4, 1975 at the Richmond Coliseum in Richmond, Virginia. Our agreement with the promoter, who needed us for ticket sales, guaranteed we could use our own monitors and be given time for a sound check. Unfortunately, Mr. Messina's marathon rehearsal went on until they opened the doors and we got screwed rock and roll style. The L&M crew, on orders from the top, refused to move any of their stage equipment to accommodate us. Our man-sized array of amplifiers and drums was squeezed into a space half of what we needed, and without a soundcheck we had no way to adjust our stage mix ahead of time. It was a recipe for audio disaster and we screwed the pooch.

From the first note to the last song of the abbreviated set, our monitors randomly howled and squealed. The band soldiered through but they were pissed. It was the absolute worst show the band and crew had endured on the tour. It was a major blemish on our winning record. As soon as we finished loading our truck after our set, JC cornered Rhyno and myself and threw a five-star English road manager wobbler. He had one point he wanted to make clear to us. Fleetwood Mac was to never be fucked out of their soundcheck again. I had never seen Courage this sincerely agitated and it was an impressive and dramatic presentation. His passion was contagious and Rhyno and I were inspired to right this wrong and restore our dignity.

The next day we played The Capitol Centre in Largo, Maryland outside of Washington D.C. Once again, we were added to a Loggins and Messina show by a promoter who didn't want to tank due to weak ticket sales. The drama of the previous day had been discussed at length by all the concerned parties and we were assured time would be made for us to check our monitors before the show. Showtime was eight p.m. and doors would open at six. We would need an hour to set up and play a couple of songs to ring the system out. The L&M band showed up at three thirty and played around for awhile without their leader. Rhyno, Mike, and I got our gear unpacked and lined up next to the stage. We persuaded our drivers and lighting guys to help us so we could get everything on stage quickly when the headliners finished their rehearsal. An hour passed and it was four forty-five with no sign of Chief Messina. If we didn't get on stage by five we would take it in the shorts again. I was starting to get heated as JC's tirade replayed in my brain.

When Jim Messina strolled on stage at four fifty-five and strapped on his guitar, I was at full boil. Rhyno and I assembled our troops and coordinated our watches. At five o'clock, our entire crew including drivers swarmed the stage from both sides and in one fell swoop set up our entire backline in front of Loggins and Messina's gear while they were playing. It was a surgical strike and the distracted players never saw it coming. The band stumbled to a halt and Jimmy lit up like a Christmas tree. He screamed for his tour manager, Jim Recor. It was at this time that Loggins' roadie Tim McCarthy came roaring up on stage and got nose to nose with me. I was fired up and having an out of body experience as my team lined up behind me in solidarity and amazement. Time stood still for a brief moment as the two most unlikely combatants on either crew prepared to take it up a notch. As if on cue, JC, Mick, and McVie arrived on stage.

Courage took one look at the scene unfolding in front of him and beamed like a proud father. Messina was apoplectic. He hadn't been told no in a long time. Now the promoter was in the mix and getting it from all sides. The warring parties moved the discussion offstage and the L&M band and crew just wandered off. That left me and my guys so we went ahead and finished our chores. We fired everything up and dialed in our sounds in an effort to beat down the feedback. JC returned with the promoter and they were yukking it up. An informal peace accord had been reached and the doors were being held until we finished our sound check. Two hours later Fleetwood Mac walked onstage to a full house of eighteen thousand. This night was a turning point. As an opener, we cut our show to an hour highlighting the crowd pleasers. The dynamics of a full set may have been compromised, but packing so many strong tunes into an hour was a big statement. A video of this show is available on YouTube. The crowd's response after *Blue Letter* says it all. We blew Loggins and Messina out of the building.

All these battles fought and won felt great. It was good to be on the winning team. After the victorious showdown with the L&M crew, our confidence was peaking. No matter what kind of train wreck greeted us during the day, we would overcome all offerings of stupidity and make the world right for the band to blow the roof off. The Mac touring party was unstoppable. It was everything I thought being on the road should be. Great music all day, everyday, and five-star male bonding at work as well as inside our rolling man cave. Unfortunately, I would soon discover there was a parallel universe of mayhem and drama that would taint my naive perception of wellbeing. I had no idea whatsoever that behind the scenes the band's personal lives were already a hot mess and just getting started. A month later I would be the last to find out that my occasional roommate, Curry Grant, was more than just friends with John's wife Christine. I was absolutely clueless. I never once thought it was odd that Christine would call our room to check on Curry and five minutes later he would be gone for the rest of the night. My lack of guile would soon be gone forever.

The only time I spent with the band on that first tour was a few hours before the show and the two hours on stage. My interaction was mostly centered around show related issues. Backstage facilities were either minimal or nonexistent and it wasn't much of a party. The band traveled on commercial flights and had already spent their day together in airports and rental cars. The mood was usually tense by the time they showed up at the venue and they all needed time to regroup and recharge. The females in the band were more likely to be approachable and engaging. As the youngest on the tour, I was treated by both women like their kid brother. I fell in love with Stevie the first day I met her and developed a high school crush of major proportion. It didn't matter that she was unavailable and out of my league. I was absolutely smitten with her.

She was a chatty gal ready to talk about most anything and I was always happy to get her attention. Christine was just as easy to be around and possessed a cool, quiet strength. She was a soulful force of nature and took no shit in the male-ruled world of rock bands.

Chris calmly stood her ground with elegance, humor, and sarcasm. The presence of two strong, smart and warm-hearted women on the road filled our daily touring life with an energy that was less cold and a little cozier than the typical boy's club scene. John was the most relatable to me of all the band members and my moral compass in a Fleetwood Mac kind of way. As Sagittarians we shared the same demented sense of humor and an analytical approach to problem solving. He was self-sufficient and not the type to clamor for attention. My kind of guy.

We had three weeks of touring left in December when Mick's guy, Mike Miller, decided he needed to go home. We had a show the next night in Dallas so Rhyno and I closed ranks and kept going on our own. Mick's kit was still normal size at this point in time and not a big deal to set up. Showtime was when the one-on-one maintenance kicked in. I was already the middle man for the monitor mixer and an able interpreter of Mick's grimaces, grunts, and scowls. He liked to be paid attention to and I was a good hand-holder. Even though I was wary of Mr. Fleetwood, I was seduced by his drive and passion. Every show was a new battle to him and he possessed a natural ability to persuade his troops to follow him into the fray with no questions asked. Rhyno and I finished up the tour as a duo. We were going into the studio in a month and would start a drum roadie search when the next tour got close.

CHAPTER 12
LB

In June 1967, San Francisco was deep in the Summer of Love. Wichita, Kansas was not. There was very little psychedelic going on in the fly-over states. Musically, the local bands were maintaining the Midwest tradition of covering R&B tunes. For us white kids that needed more soul, this was how we first learned about real music. One day early in summer vacation between seventh and eighth grade, I was riding my bike in the neighborhood cruising for potential lawns to mow. From behind the garage door of Jimmy Hill's house came a rumbling noise that sounded vaguely familiar but was not immediately recognizable. It was a guitar, bass, and drums chugging out something like *Mustang Sally.* When the singing started I knew for sure it was the Wilson Pickett workhorse. I peeked in the window and was amazed to see Mike and Gary Wall on four and six-string and the quiet Jimmy Hill kicking it strong on a big boy pro drum kit. A single Silvertone amp was handling the bass, electric guitar, and vocal mic.

It sounded good to me and was quite a revelation as I had no idea of my straight-laced classmate's double identity. I invited myself in and sat on the gray two-speaker Sears guitar amp. It emitted a warm sweet aroma that was a mixture of cheap capacitors, overheated tubes, and a too small transformer. It was an exotic and earthy blend created by old school electronics being pushed over the edge. The smell coupled with the sound, and I was quite taken by my first taste of a live band experienced at ground zero. In cool rock style, the guys tolerated my intrusion with low key indifference. They played eight or nine more tunes, mostly Sam and Dave, Motown, and Mr. Pickett—I knew all the songs—they were the bread and butter of the church dance band I'd go see on Saturday nights. They quit for the day and we all got on our bikes and went home.

That night I pulled out my trumpet and worked up a horn chart for *Hold On I'm Coming.* The next day I returned to the garage with my axe and just joined in. No one asked me to leave so I figured I was in the band. For a month I hung out and put brass parts on half a dozen more soul revue dance tunes. The image of twelve year old freckle-faced Gary Wall belting out "I'm a soul man" is a forever memory. Everything seemed to be going in a positive direction until I got my first taste of the dark side of show business. When I found out that my colleagues had played their first paying gig at the church without me, I swore off musicians and bands and put my horn away for the rest of the summer.

It was just a few weeks later when I picked up my first acoustic guitar and began pursuing my musical calling as a lone wolf. My dis-enchantment was perfectly suited for songs of protest, broken hearts, and disappointment. I was cruising along pretty happily as a purist folkie finger-picker until I heard Eric Clapton and wanted to be him. All the premier contemporary blues rock guitarists played with a pick so I found a plectrum and started wood shedding. I thought I would be ripping some tasty lead guitar in no time but it never kicked in for me. I tried and tried but a flat pick just never felt comfortable. I'm sure it would have helped if I had an electric guitar and amp, but I was on my own and didn't know better. I returned to my Travis picking and sur-rendered to the reality that I would probably not be a note shredding, string bending, guitar gun slinger. I would have to share my musical gifts in a manner more suited to my demeanor and skills.

The first night I saw Lindsey Buckingham playing his song *So Afraid was* a revelation. He clearly possessed the essential gifts of the holiest of guitar gods, and all with his naked thumb and fingers. Down the line, I would learn that there were a number of blues guys playing bad ass electric guitar without a pick but seeing and hearing Lindsey tear it up in that style was a moment of sweet discovery. It was empowering to rise above my preconceptions of what could and couldn't be done. It was also the beginning of Lindsey opening my eyes and heart to the sacred world of creativity. For every "right" way of doing something there could be a dozen "not right" ways as well. Out of these left turns and happy accidents appear surprise destinations that aren't even being sought.

My first six months with Fleetwood Mac I was reborn as a guitarist and began to learn what it was to be a musician. The previous year I had stopped playing music completely and now I was around guitars all day long and could play anytime. The band would arrive at the venue around five or six after flying and driving all day. Lindsey, desperate for time away from the traveling party, would want a quiet place to warm up before showtime. I would greet him with a joint and take him to whatever out of the way space I had found for the day. Echoey tiled showers were preferred. For the next hour he would let me hang out while he noodled and decompressed. I had never sat across from an accomplished guitarist and studied what he did while I listened. I learned about hammer ons and offs, open tunings, capos, chord inversions, and on and on. He would randomly drift between blues, country, folk, or classical styles. I would hear riffs or chord changes that in weeks or years would become fully produced recordings.

Some of my favorite pieces were show tunes that I recognized from my Dad's song-books. It was the ultimate learning tool to see fingers on a fretboard playing notes that I had watched Pop play on a keyboard. Lindsey loved standards as much as my dad and I. It was Lindsey's dad, Buck, that opened his youngest son's ears to those same tunes. Besides two hours onstage, this was the only time I spent with LB that first year. Through our many subsequent years together he exposed me to songwriting, arranging, and editing. He taught me about recording, overdubbing, bouncing, and mixing. He showed me how to make his studio work and I taught myself how to keep it working.

LB

There was only one time I would ever see Lindsey struggle with playing a guitar. The band's oldest fans were all devotees of Mac founding member Peter Green. It was important to pay tribute to the revered guitarist and include some of his best known tunes in the band's set. *Oh Well was* one of the original band's signature songs and showcased some of Greenie's most dazzling and iconic riffs. Every night Lindsey aptly replicated the fan favorite but was still working out the technique required to finger-pick guitar runs originally played with a flat pick. This was high energy dramatic rock guitar and demanded over the top commitment from the player. Every now and then, LB would lose his grip on the wheel and the clams would go flying. Mick would take these bumps in the road the hardest and for a few weeks embarked on a campaign to persuade Lindsey to start using a pick. This was not received well by the newest player in the band and on a couple of occasions, pushed him to briefly quit the quintet. The perfectionist in Lindsey was hurting bad on this one, but his swim team stubbornness prevailed and he soon conquered the pesky cover tune his way.

"Don't ask me what I think of you
I might not give the answer that you want me to…"

Oh Well
Peter Green

CHAPTER 13
AC COBRA

In January 1976 Rhyno and I loaded up a rental truck with Fleetwood Mac's instruments, amps, and drums and took a drive up the coast to the Record Plant in Sausalito, CA. This was a new recording studio that combined the best equipment with the finest creature comforts in pursuit of elevating the aesthetics of the recording process. Most studios up to this point were either sterile facilities run by guys in lab coats, or large broom closets with egg cartons tacked to the walls for soundproofing. The Record Plant franchise believed in making their clients very comfortable while making great sounding records and was already operating successful facilities in New York and Los Angeles. The Northern California version of their business model was in Sausalito, a charming tourist town just over the Golden Gate Bridge. Nestled in Marin County, the area just north of San Francisco was the new destination for the Bay Area music scene after the Haight-Ashbury went sour. It was 1970's affluent hippie nirvana. The rolling hills and gorgeous redwoods were filled with A-frames, Porsches, and a record number of drug dealers per capita. In the heart of the community at 2200 Bridgeway was the redwood-paneled Record Plant.

One of the top four studios in the Bay Area, every musician in town had done some kind of work there. This spawned an informal open door policy that turned the place into a clubhouse for all with sufficient hipness or connectivity to hang out. Cosmic chaos was a frequent visitor and often stayed longer than desired. Prior to our stay, it is told, the studio would obtain industrial grade nitrous oxide under the pretext that it was required to keep the tape machines cool. Gas masks hung from the ceiling for those looking for a quick one but over indulgence and lack of supervision put an end to this practice.

This was my first time in a recording studio and this place was a trip. There was a private jacuzzi and a conference room with a water-bed floor. Sly Stone had a custom sunken floor studio called "The Pit." Chefs were on call to prepare whatever meals were desired at any time. Another feature for out of town clients was the use of a guest-house in nearby Mill Valley. A four-bedroom ranch style house with minimal furnishings served as the men's dormitory. Myself, Rhyno, Ken Caillat, Richard Dashut, Lindsey, and John McVie made it our home for the duration. The house also caught the overflow of any out of town guests like road manager JC, or photographer, Herbie Worthington. Mick rented a place down the road for himself, wife Jenny and daughters Amy and Lucy. Christine and Stevie stayed at a two-bedroom condo in Tiburon.

After Rhyno and I set up all the gear in the studio, we served our time primarily as babysitters and chauffeurs. After six months of single-handedly juggling the well being of five musicians in various stages of breakup, JC handed the keys to the asylum over to his road crew. There was some random equipment maintenance and daily guitar string changing, but for the most part we were shuttling band members between the studio and their respective lodgings. Mick and Jenny were trying to patch up their marriage, John and Christine were getting divorced, and Lindsey and Stevie had just broken up. It was a constant in and out of players depending on who was talking to who. Adding to this complexity was the need to keep everyone in the studio at one time as we were there to cut basic tracks. This process is usually most fruitful when the whole band participates.

Ken had his car with him and Richard traveled with LB in his car. Everybody else was without wheels so Rhyno and I went car shopping for something we could pick the band up in as well as carry gear. My partner fell in love with a bright orange used Datsun pickup. It had huge tires with chrome wheels and resembled a Mattel Hot Wheels toy truck. With a standard transmission and seemingly no suspension, it was perfect for a couple of flatland hipsters out on the town. As a band limo it sucked. John McVie never complained about it. He appreciated the low key profile and the money-saving four-cylinder engine. The girls hated it. The springs were so tight that every time we would hit a big bump, our heads would slam in the roof. Whoever sat in the middle, usually the shorter Stevie, would have their knees pummeled by the gear shift every time I went to second or fourth.

They were extra repulsed by the orange paint job. It was the car conscious Mick Fleetwood who suffered the most while traveling in the non-deluxe rice burner. Mick has had a lifelong passion for quality conveyances and the unruly Datsun challenged his motoring and style sensibilities. Everyday I would go get Mick to take him to the studio. It was a short ride on the 101 North to the Fleetwood family compound. Right off the freeway by his apartment was a boutique car dealership. There were only a few dozen pieces there but they were all high-end previously owned cars. Mostly Porsches and Mercedes with the odd Ferrari and Aston Martin thrown in. However, the car that caught Mick's eye was parked up front on an elevated metal ramp. It was a pristine original Shelby AC Cobra. A hybrid of the English AC hand-built racing car and a Ford engine, the Cobra was the dream of American car builder Carroll Shelby. Mick knew everything about them and each time we drove by he would softly moan his appreciation to himself. I had heard Mick make these noises before but only when he was playing drums.

One day after picking up my drummer I was instructed to drive past the freeway on-ramp and into the car lot. The arrival of the orange Datsun did nothing to capture the attention of the salesman inside. This changed when the six-foot-six nattily attired Englishman unfolded himself from my tiny cab and strode towards the object of his desire. Mick calmly informed the salesman that he would be purchasing the Cobra today and would like it brought down the ramp. He then pulled an Elvis-sized wad of cash out of his tailored jeans pocket to demonstrate the seriousness of his intentions. The car was gently backed down and parked in front us. Mick slowly circled the Shelby and opened the driver's door. He was so happy. Serious and long-delayed satisfaction would soon be his. Ken Caillat had just purchased a Mercedes and this acquisition would put Mick back on top.

AC Cobra

Sadly, victory would not be his today. Despite numerous attempts to squeeze into the pilot's position, a roll bar welded to the frame behind the drivers seat stopped the extra tall Brit from moving back far enough to get his legs under the steering wheel. There were long faces all around. No cool car for Mick. No tasty commission for the salesman. Offers of Porsches and Ferraris were extended but Mick was inconsolable. There would be no replacement for the fabulous Cobra today. There was nothing left to do but get back in the orange Datsun and head back to the studio of pain and heartbreak.

Bigger than the personal storm clouds shrouding the studio was the presence of magical, moody music in every room at all times of the day. These were five inspired creative people stitching together an amazing quilt of songs and everyday was filled with their playing and singing. From Stevie writing *Dreams* on an electric piano in Sly Stone's shag-carpeted man cave to Christine's recording of *Songbird* on a nine-foot Steinway grand piano at Zellerbach Auditorium, Fleetwood Mac music was being pursued with a vengeance. After six months of epic live shows and three months inside the bubble that spawned *Rumours,* there was no consideration on my part of being anywhere else. It was uncharted, unruly, and unpredictable but continued to be filled with endless possibility. There was no way to not stay to see what was going to happen next. The Fleetwood Mac modus operandi was becoming a way of life and our unplanned template for group success.

One of the main downsides for me was to be saturated by the details of the personal lives of my employers everyday. I don't know how JC survived it and now knew why he sent me and Rhyno to San Francisco in his place. We needed to get back on the road where there were some personal boundaries and monitored visitation periods. It was time for Courage to take them back.

1976 SUMMER TOUR
APRIL

22	FRESNO CA LIFORNIA	SELLAND ARENA
23	PHOENIX ARIZONA	CIVIC PLAZA
24		
25	OAKLAND CALIFORNIA	OAKLAND STADIUM
26	LAS VEGAS NEVADA	CONVENTION CENTER
27	LOS ANGELES CALIFORNIA	LOYOLA MARYMOUNT COLLEGE
28	RENO NEVADA	RENO CENTENNIAL COLISEUM
29	CHICO CALIFORNIA	CHICO STATE UNIVERSITY STADIUM

MAY 1976

01	OAKLAND CALIFORNIA	OAKLAND STADIUM
02	SANTA BARBARA CALIFORNIA	UCSB STADIUM

JUNE 1976

18	KANSAS CITY MISSOURI	ROYALS STADIUM
19	OMAHA NEBRASKA	OMAHA ARENA
20	DES MOINES IOWA	IOWA STATE FAIRGROUNDS
21	CLARKSTON MICHIGAN	PINE KNOB MUSIC THEATER
22	CLARKSTON MICHIGAN	PINE KNOB MUSIC THEATER
23		
24	MILWAUKEE WISCONSIN	MILWAUKEE ARENA
25	PEORIA ILLINOIS	GLEN OAK PARK
26	MINNEAPOLIS MINNESOTA	PARADE STADIUM
27	FARGO NORTH DAKOTA	NORTH DAKOTA UNIV. STADIUM

28
29 ST. LOUIS MISSOURI   BUSCH STADIUM
30 CINCINNATI OHIO   RIVERFRONT COLISEUM

JULY 1976

01
02 GREENSBORO NORTH CAROLINA GREENSBORO
           COLISEUM
03 ATLANTA GEORGIA   THE OMNI
04 TAMPA FLORIDA   STADIUM
05 JACKSONVILLE FLORIDA JACKSONVILLE
           COLISEUM
06 TO 11   MIAMI FLORIDA
           CRITERIA RECORDING
           STUDIO
12 PHILADELPHIA PENNSYLVANIA THE SPECTRUM
13 SYRACUSE PENNSYLVANIA WAR MEMORIAL
           COLISEUM
14 HARTFORD CONNECTICUT COLT PARK
15
16 GREEN BAY WISCONSIN BROWN COUNTY
           ARENA
17 MADISON WISCONSIN   DANE COUNTY ARENA
18 DENVER COLORADO   MILE HIGH STADIUM
19 WICHITA KANSAS   HENRY LEVITT ARENA
20
21 HOMEWOOD ILLINOIS   WASHINGTON PARK
22
23 RICHFIELD OHIO   RICHFIELD COLISEUM
24 PITTSBURGH PENNSYLVANIA THREE RIVERS
           STADIUM
25 FOXBORO MASSACHUSETTS FOXBORO STADIUM
26
27 LARGO MARYLAND   CAPITAL CENTRE

AUGUST 1976

24	SAN BERNARDINO CALIFORNIA	SWING AUDITORIUM
25	SAN DIEGO CALIFORNIA	SPORTS ARENA
26		
27	LOS ANGELES CALIFORNIA	UNIVERSAL AMPHITHEATER
28	LOS ANGELES CALIFORNIA	UNIVERSAL AMPHITHEATER
29	LOS ANGELES CALIFORNIA	UNIVERSAL AMPHITHEATER
30	LOS ANGELES CALIFORNIA	UNIVERSAL AMPHITHEATER

SEPTEMBER 1976

05	AUSTIN TEXAS	STEINER RANCH

CHAPTER 14
TAKE 2 ASPIRIN

In April 1976 we closed up shop at the Record Plant and set out on tour. Our road credibility had vastly improved from the last time we were out just four months earlier. The Fleetwood Mac "White Album" was headed to No.1 on the Billboard charts and we were now selling out the same arenas that had us as the support act the year before. Everyone was making money and road accommodations had been upgraded. The band was now traveling in their own private plane and JC had enlisted handlers to road manage the daily needs of his charges.

Courage made sure each band member had equal access to all amenities in an effort to keep what little peace there was. The initial trauma and pain of everyone's uncouplings had peaked, but now the band entered their next phase of raw nerves and confrontation. New romantic partners were traveling as part of the entourage with predictably mixed results. Their long-fought career success had finally arrived and now everyone was seeking a little satisfaction in their personal lives. Once again, the relative safest and happiest place in the day was showtime on stage.

Towards the end of the three-month summer tour we played the Spectrum in Philadelphia. Home to 76er's pro basketball and Flyers hockey, the arena was also across the street from Veterans Stadium where the Phillies played baseball. The afternoon of the show, I took a cab downtown to stock up on guitar strings at a music store. An early game had just finished and the street was filled with baseball fans trying to get back downtown. My driver asked if I minded sharing a fare and I agreed. We stopped for two middle aged gentlemen flagging us down. They both were sporting American Legion colors and were headed to the majestic Stratford-Bellevue Hotel. My driver said it was right by my music store and we welcomed them aboard. Traffic started to get heavy and our trip ended up taking about forty-five minutes. We dropped them off and my cabbie waited while I ran in to pick up my order. I made it back for sound check and we cruised through another sold out show.

Two weeks later the summer leg of our tour came to a close at the Capital Centre in Largo, Maryland. Getting off the bus for awhile was always a good excuse to get the party started. Early flights home and rooms at the band's hotel were all that was needed to bypass going to bed that night. By noon I was back in Hermosa Beach looking and feeling like I had been on the road for three months. Happy but well used.

Our monitor engineer, Ken D'Alessandro, picked up another tour at the last minute and let me stay at his apartment. After an extended run on a bus with eleven guys, I was craving some solitude. I went grocery shopping and settled in for a full lockdown. A little Monday afternoon nap turned into a long one as two days of abandon caught up to me. At nine p.m. I awoke drenched in sweat with a fever and body aches. After a handful of aspirin and a half gallon of water I spent the rest of the night racked with flu symptoms. It would not be the first time I had come home from a long road trip and have my body turn on me. Hopefully this would burn out in a day or two and not completely ruin my week off. Tuesday crawled into Wednesday and things were not improving. I couldn't eat and my fever was still hanging on.

I moved out to the couch to smoke some hash and watch the news. After three months in a roadie submarine you lose touch with things like current events and world affairs. Walter Cronkite and the CBS News opened with an update on a situation that had apparently been perplexing authorities for a few days. There was a strange epidemic breaking out in the northeastern U.S. A number of middle-aged men in the New York, Boston, and Philadelphia area were developing flu-like illnesses with some dying. There were no clues as to a cause or if these cases were even related. The broadcast moved onto oil problems and sketchy politicians. Obviously, I wasn't the only one feeling like shit.

Mark Drale and Kenny D'Alessandro

On Thursday, Kenny calls to tell me he wouldn't be home for another week. I told him that was just as well as I was down for the count and most likely contagious. I hung up the phone and switched on the TV for my nightly national news fix. Once again, the lead story focused on the lengthening list of unexplainable illnesses on the East Coast. There seemed to be only one common thread so far. All of the deceased, now numbering five, had been members of the American Legion. The Legion was a government sponsored organization created after WWI to be a social safety net for active and retired armed forces personnel. A TV pundit suggested they could be victims of a germ warfare attack orchestrated by anti government factions wound up by the country's two-hundredth birthday celebration. I was sympathetic and curious but had my own germs to wallow in.

It's now Friday and I'm trying to recall if I have ever been this ill for this length of time. I am beginning to seriously consider doing something I hadn't done since I was fourteen years old—go to a doctor. I showered, drank some apple juice, and laid back down on the couch pathetically moaning to myself. Mindless television viewing was my only solace so I found Channel 7 and settled in for some *All My Children.* Ten minutes in and my mental hiatus was put on hold. Regular programming was being interrupted for an important news bulletin.

Five more deaths had occurred overnight and over eighty others were ill with the same symptoms. I was now officially on fatal flu watch. This is before twenty-four-hour cable news and Ken's TV was not remote friendly. I made a pallet on the floor close to the set so I could reach the knob for quick channel changing. The rest of the day was a blur. My five day fever had beaten me down and I was wiped out as I switched from channel to channel.

The Big Three networks were all breaking into their daytime shows for updates and speculations. Over and over, images of the departed appeared on the screen. A wide spectrum of potential theories were taking shape and an underlying tone of paranoia was starting to creep in. Was it Swine Flu? Bacterial warfare? Had the water supply been compromised? Experts from the CIA and the Center for Disease Control debated the numerous ways the population of the U.S. could be efficiently exterminated. Interspersed between these reports were grim announcements of another passing or more poor souls falling ill. I watched all night enthralled with the real life *Twilight Zone* sucking in the whole country.

The final broadcast of the evening delivered a crushing blow as the whole mess suddenly got personal. Government germ detectives had just announced a breakthrough. Not only was every victim an American Legion member, they had all attended the same huge event together. The next image glowing on the tube was a picture of the Stratford-Bellevue Hotel in downtown Philadelphia, site of their recent convention and probable ground zero. I recognized it immediately as the local landmark that was the destination of my American Legion cab mates two weeks earlier when I went shopping at the nearby music store. The network signed off for the night as did the other news outlets. All that was left was test patterns, white noise, and my racing mind. I couldn't stop thinking about the forty-five minutes I had spent in a poorly air-conditioned taxi with two potentially infectious Legionnaires. That would seem to be plenty of time to suck in any death-inducing spores that might be coughed my way.

For five days, I had been majorly sick with every symptom that had taken down or killed almost a hundred people. Two weeks earlier, I had spent almost an hour with probable carriers in close quarters and traveled with them to the crime scene. This was feeling like it could be a real problem. I finally passed out around two a.m. on the couch and had some really messed up dreams. The television woke me when the morning news returned with a vengeance. Three more fatalities had occurred overnight. That was it. It was time to seek professional medical advice. The few guys I knew living nearby were out of town so I called a taxi and made my way to the South Bay Hospital emergency room.

I approached the admitting desk with apprehension. The nurse eyeballed me and inquired as to the nature of my issues. I explained my six days of flu symptoms but stopped at what I feared was the real problem. I wanted to see a doctor before I spilled my guts. Since I didn't have a gunshot wound or severed limb, I sat in the waiting room for two hours. My name was eventually called and I was sent to an exam room where an overworked and sleep-deprived intern sat down in front of me. Unshaven and sporting a poorly groomed seventies white man afro, I unraveled the timeline and history of my last couple of weeks. I briefed him on the mystery plague sweeping the East Coast and my contact with likely front line carriers. It was highly possible that I could be the source of potential infection of the entire West Coast. A wave of relief washed over me as I surrendered myself to the healing hands of this highly trained representative of the professional medical community. My brain was in overdrive as I prepared myself for whatever might be coming next. Lab tests? Isolation ward? FBI interviews? Who knew? We were traveling in unexplored territory.

My angel of mercy finished his notes on a clipboard and slowly stood up. He pulled an unmarked bottle from a drawer, turned to me and somberly offered me two pills. "You have the flu. Take these aspirin and go to bed. Please go now." He opened the door and waved to security. After confirming I had sufficient funds for transportation I was escorted to the curb and placed in a taxi. Clearly my presentation had failed to ignite any sense of crisis or fear. I was deemed irrelevant and sent back under whatever rock I shared with the other ne'er-do-well street urchins.

Back in Kenny's guest room, I lay spent from days of viral battering and no food or real sleep. I called the few people I knew in town again to come help me but no one was around. I closed my eyes, sighed a deep breath, and fell into a long, uninterrupted slumber. Twenty hours later I awoke to the ringing phone. It was road manager John Courage rested and refreshed after six days in Maui. Ken Caillat had just booked time at Wally Heider's studio and I was the only one around to collect the band's gear and get it set up. I hung up the phone and realized I was not only not dead, I wasn't shivering with fever and was really hungry. It was a Fleetwood Mac miracle. I showered, ate, and returned to the studio where we would spend five more months finishing the recording and mixing of *"Rumours"*. Back in the Fleetwood Mac bubble, I soon lost track again of life on the outside. We had become proficient at cultivating our own reality and there was little time for the regular world.

Some time later, the cause of the mysterious illnesses and deaths originating from the Bellevue- Stratford Hotel In Philadelphia was discovered. The ancient heating ducts had spawned a deadly bacteria that was spread throughout the structure when the air conditioning was turned on. In the end, two hundred and eleven people fell ill and twenty-nine died. This was the first known outbreak of what is now known as Legionnaire's Disease. Another Forrest Gump brush with history.

RUMOURS TOUR
FEBRUARY 1977

02 *RUMOURS* RELEASED

28 BERKELEY CA — BERKELEY COMMUNITY THEATER

29 SAN DIEGO CA — SPORTS ARENA

MARCH 1977

03 EL PASO TEXAS — COLISEUM

04 ALBUQUERQUE NEW MEXICO — UNIVERSITY OF NEW MEXICO ARENA

05 LUBBOCK TEXAS — COLISEUM

06 FT. WORTH TEXAS — TARRANT COUNTY CONVENTION CTR

07 HOUSTON TEXAS — THE SUMMIT

08

09 OKLAHOMA CITY OKLAHOMA — FAIRGROUNDS ARENA

10 TULSA OKLAHOMA — ASSEMBLY CENTER

11 LITTLE ROCK ARKANSAS — BARTON COLISEUM

12 BIRMINGHAM ALABAMA — BIRMINGHAM JEFFERSON COLISEUM

13 CHARLOTTE NORTH CAROLINA

14

15 COLUMBIA SOUTH CAROLINA — CAROLINA COLISEUM

16 KNOXVILLE TENNESEE — CIVIC CENTER

17 RICHMOND VIRGINIA — RICHMOND COLISEUM

18 NORFOLK VIRGINIA — THE SCOPE

19 GREENSBORO NORTH CAROLINA — COLISEUM

APRIL 1977

02 BIRMINGHAM ENGLAND — ODEON THEATER

03

04 GLASGOW SCOTLAND — APOLLO CENTER

05 MANCHESTER ENGLAND — APOLLO CENTER

06	BRISTOL ENGLAND	COLSTON ENGLAND
07		
08	LONDON ENGLAND	RAINBOW THEATER
09	LONDON ENGLAND	RAINBOW THEATER
10	LONDON ENGLAND	RAINBOW THEATER
11		
12	PARIS FRANCE	PAVILLION
13	AMSTERDAM HOLLAND	NIEU RAI
14	FRANKFURT GERMANY	STADTHALLE
15	MUNICH GERMANY	CIRCUS KRONE
16	HAMBURG GERMANY	CONGRESS CENTER
17		
29	SALT LAKE CITY UTAH	SPECIAL EVENTS CENTER
30		

MAY 1977

01	BOULDER COLORADO	UNIVERSITY OF COLORADO
02	LARAMIE WYOMING	WYOMING UNIVERSITY FIELDHOUSE
03	BILLINGS MONTANA	METRO ARENA
05		
06		
07	OAKLAND CALIFORNIA	OAKLAND STADIUM
08	SANTA BARBARA CALIFORNIA	UCSB STADIUM
09		
10	ALBUQUERQUE NEW MEXICO	UNIVERSITY OF NEW MEXICO
11	EL PASO TEXAS	EL PASO COLISEUM
12		
13		
14	HOUSTON TEXAS	THE SUMMIT

15 FT. WORTH TEXAS   TARRANT COUNTY CONVENTION CTR

16

17

18 OKLAHOMA CITY OKLAHOMA   FAIRGROUNDS ARENA

19 TULSA OKLAHOMA   ASSEMBLY CENTER

20 LITTLE ROCK ARKANSAS   BARTON COLISEUM

21 NASHVILLE TENNESSEE   MUNICIPAL AUDITORIUM

22

23

24 COLUMBIA SOUTH CAROLINA   CAROLINA COLISEUM

25 CHARLOTTE NORTH CAROLINA   CHARLOTTE COLISEUM

26

27

28 MIAMI FLORIDA   BASEBALL STADIUM

29 ORLANDO FLORIDA   TANGERINE BOWL

30

31

JUNE 1977

01 ATLANTA GEORGIA   THE OMNI

02 BIRMINGHAM ALABAMA   BIRMINGHAM/ JEFFERSON COLISEUM

03 MEMPHIS TENNESSEE   MID SOUTH COLISEUM

04

05 NEW ORLEANS LOUISIANA   TAD GORMLEY STADIUM

27 BINGHAMTON NEW YORK   BROOME COUNTY ARENA

28 SYRACUSE NEW YORK   WAR MEMORIAL ARENA

29	NEW YORK CITY NEW YORK	MADISON SQUARE GARDEN
30	NEW YORK CITY NEW YORK	MADISON SQUARE GARDEN

JULY 1977

01		
02	BUFFALO NEW YORK	WAR MEMORIAL ARENA
03	BUFFALO NEW YORK	WAR MEMORIAL ARENA
04	TORONTO CANADA	CNE
05		
06		
07	PROVIDENCE RHODE ISLAND	CIVIC CENTER
08		
09	CHARLOTTE NORTH CAROLINA	COLISEUM
10	RICHMOND VIRGINIA	COLISEUM
11	NORFOLK VIRGINIA	THE SCOPE
12	LARGO MARYLAND	CAPITAL CENTER
13	LARGO MARYLAND	CAPITAL CENTER
14		
15	CHARLESTON WEST VIRGINIA	
16	LEXINGTON KENTUCKY	
17		
18	CLARKSTON MICHIGAN	PINE KNOB
19	CLARKSTON MICHIGAN	PINE KNOB
20	CLARKSTON MICHIGAN	PINE KNOB
21	CLARKSTON MICHIGAN	PINE KNOB
22		
23	CHICAGO ILLINOIS	CHICAGO STADIUM
24	CHICAGO ILLINOIS	CHICAGO STADIUM

AUGUST 1977

24	LAS VEGAS NEVADA	ALADDIN THEATER
25	LAS VEGAS NEVADA	ALADDIN THEATER

26
27 TUCSON ARIZONA   TUCSON STADIUM
28
29 LOS ANGELES CALIFORNIA   THE FORUM
30 LOS ANGELES CALIFORNIA   THE FORUM
31 LOS ANGELES CALIFORNIA   THE FORUM

SEPTEMBER 1977

01
02 SEATTLE WASHINGTON   COLISEUM
03 SEATTLE WASHINGTON   COLISEUM
04 PORTLAND OREGON   COLISEUM
05 VANCOUVER CANADA   PNE
06
07 CALGARY CANADA   STAMPEDE GRANDSTAND
08 EDMONTON CANADA   COLISEUM
09
10
11 MILWAUKEE WISCONSIN   MILWAUKEE COUNTY
                                  STADIUM
12 ST. PAUL MINNESITA   CIVIC AUDITORIUM
13
14 OMAHA NEBRASKA   CIVIC CENTER
15
16 ST. LOUIS MISSOURI   KIEL AUDITORIUM
17 KANSAS CITY MISSOURI   KEMPER AUDITORIUM
18
19
20 INDIANAPOLIS INDIANA   MARKET SQUARE ARENA
21 LOUISVILLE KENTUCKY   FREEDOM HALL
22
23
24 DETROIT MICHIGAN   COBO ARENA
25 RICHFIELD OHIO   RICHFIELD COLISEUM

26	RICHFIELD OHIO	RICHFIELD COLISEUM
27	PHILADELPHIA PENNSYLVANIA	THE SPECTRUM
28		
29		
30		

OCTOBER 1977

01		
02	SANTA BARBARA CALIFORNIA	STADIUM UCSB
03		
04	SAN DIEGO CALIFORNIA	SPORTS ARENA

NOVEMBER 1977

11	SYDNEY AUSTRALIA	SYDNEY SHOW GROUNDS
12		
13	MELBOURNE AUSTRALIA	CALDER RACEWAY
14		
15	BRISBANE AUSTRALIA	FESTIVAL HALL
16	BRISBANE AUSTRALIA	FESTIVAL HALL
17		
18	PERTH AUSTRALIA	ENTERTAINMENT CENTER
19	PERTH AUSTRALIA	ENTERTAINMENT CENTER
20		
21		
22		
23	ADELAIDE AUSTRALIA	ADELAIDE OVAL
24		
25		
26		
27	AUCKLAND NEW ZEALAND	WESTERN SPRINGS STADIUM

28
29
30

DECEMBER 1977

01
02 NAGOYA JAPAN   NAGOYA SHI KOKAIDO
03 OSAKA JAPAN   EXPO HALL
04 OSAKA JAPAN   EXPO HALL
05 TOKYO JAPAN   THE BUDOKAN
06
07 HONOLULU HAWAII   BLAISDELL ARENA
08 HONOLULU HAWAII   BLAISDELL ARENA
09
10 LAHAINA MAUI HAWAII   ROYAL LAHAINA TENNIS
                                     STADIUM

JULY 1978

17 EAST TROY WISCONSIN   ALPINE VALLEY MUSIC
                                     THEATER
18 EAST TROY WISCONSIN   ALPINE VALLEY MUSIC
                                     THEATER
19 EAST TROY WISCONSIN   ALPINE VALLEY MUSIC
                                     THEATER
20
21 BOULDER COLORADO   FOLSOM STADIUM
22
23 DALLAS TEXAS   COTTON BOWL
24
25
26 SARATOGA SPRINGS NEW YORK   PERFORMING ARTS
                                     CENTER
27
28 BUFFALO NEW YORK   RICH STADIUM

29

30 PHILADELPHIA PENNSYLVANIA   JFK STADIUM

AUGUST 1978

24 LEXINGTON KENTUCKY   RUPP ARENA

25

26 CLEVELAND OHIO   MUNICIPAL STADIUM

27

28 BIRMINGHAM ALABAMA   JEFFERSON STADIUM

29 ATLANTA GEORGIA   THE OMNI

30 BATON ROUGE LOUISIANA   CENTROPLEX ARENA

CHAPTER 15
GO YOUR OWN WAY

Lindsey Buckingham's *Rumours* classic, *Go Your Own Way,* has had an impact on my life since the song's beginnings. I first heard the original form the same time as the rest of the band in November 1975. On a short break toward the end of a five-month tour, we rented a house by a swamp near Homestead outside of Miami, Florida. The semi-truck was parked out front and we filled the living room with our drums, keyboards, and amplifiers. The crew camped out in the house and the band would drive out everyday from their hotel in Miami to work on new material for their next album. It was an informal gathering and the Fleetwood Mac way of taking time off. The three songwriters all had seeds of song ideas for their next album and the band would jam and see where it took them. Lindsey's first contribution was well-formed and band-ready. It was a stripped down and straight-ahead arrangement that was equal parts electric guitar, bass, and drums. The most obvious quality was a pronounced aggressive attitude with less than gracious lyrics directed at Stevie.

A few months later we were at the Record Plant in Sausalito turning those demos from the Homestead house into basic tracks for the next album. Most of the males in our party stayed ten minutes away at the studio's guest house in Mill Valley. Lindsey, Richard, and I were usually the first ones up and would start the day listening to music while enjoying a morning wake and bake. There was a modest stereo in the living room with a small random collection of records. The Rolling Stones' *Beggars Banquet was* a favorite and the Charlie Watts toms on *Street Fighting Man* inspired the vibe for Mick's drum pattern on *Go Your Own Way.*

Later that year at Wally Heider Studios in Hollywood, LB would add the counterpoint acoustic guitar that opens the song. When the guitar lead takes off at the end of the song, the rhythm guitar couples with Mick's drums and John's bass to keep the tune driving into rock immortality.

February 1977 the *Rumours* album is released as well as the first single, *Go Your Own Way.* Months have been spent layering and doubling instruments, especially guitars, to achieve the rich, full, Grammy-winning sound. Fleetwood Mac with Lindsey, Ken, and Richard producing, have crafted a sonic masterpiece. It was time for one of the strongest live acts on the road to take it to the people. The next order of business was a couple weeks of rehearsals to put the new songs into the set.

The band was blessed with the ability of taking their recorded tracks to the stage with just their four instruments and three voices without losing anything in translation. The power of the group playing live took the already strong material to another level and the Mac faithful worshipped the group's stage chemistry. Having two distinct guitar parts in the same song presented a new challenge for Lindsey. The acoustic rhythm guitar that he added in the studio was not only the signature sound that started the song, but part of the foundation for the electric solo going out. Lindsey wanted both parts on stage and needed a second player. He set his sights on Stevie who wrote songs on guitar and accompanied herself when singing. This was going to be a tricky negotiation. Stevie already hated the lyrics about her "shacking up" and there was no clear reason for her to show any vulnerability to her on-again, off-again nemesis. Somehow Lindsey broke through and and she agreed to give it a shot. The group took a break in their rehearsals for the guitar player to teach his ex-girlfriend her guitar part.

Magically, the two began to bond and share pleasant musical memories. An unexpected positive vibe took the room by surprise and everyone welcomed the friendly spirits. After half an hour of private tutoring, Buckingham and Nicks returned to their places on stage with their bandmates. Mick slapped his kick while guitar and drums meshed to set the beat and start the intro. Lindsey locked eyes with Stevie and started the count for her cue to begin. For the next ten minutes the band executed one false start after another as the singer struggled to hit the entry point for her part. To Lindsey, finding the turned-around beat was second nature. The fact that it was a little weird is what made it good, but also not easily grasped by Stephanie. Lindsey's veiled patience was vaporizing and Stevie was beginning to melt down in an uncomfortable way. A familiar tension returned to the musty room.

Stevie's brief tenure as Fleetwood Mac guitarist

My outpost during this entire exchange was by the monitor mixer on stage left, about ten feet away. As the final false start begins, Lindsey catches me trying to help his struggling guitarist count in and find the entry point. When the Stevie train leaves the track for the last time, LB takes the guitar from her, walks over to me and lays it in my lap. He turns back to Stevie and says, "Raymond can play this better than you!"

I knew this was more of a rebuke to Stevie than an endorsement of my musicianship. Lindsey was on a mission and he wasn't leaving until he got what he wanted. He sat down next to me and began to teach me the elusive part. The song was in the key of "F" but Lindsey put a capo on the eighth fret and showed me what to play starting with an "A" chord. It made the basic I IV V pattern an "A," "D," and "E" for the verses and "F#m," "D," and "E" for the chorus and solo out.

I could find the chords okay but strumming with a pick was another trip entirely. I played finger-style guitar. I had rhythm but not with a plectrum. I was sucking bad. In spite of what had just gone down in the room with Stevie, Lindsey was patient and cool with me. We sat together and he played me through my spastic shuffle-like strum and got me to feel the strident on top of the beat attack. He stayed with me and we played the simple figure over and over and over until I finally started to relax into it. Then, out of nowhere, Mick slid into place and the rest of the band joined in with him. It was primitive but cool. I held on all the way through to the end of the pass and even got an "All right Raymond" from Christine. The band called it a night and everybody headed out as I sat in amused disbelief. Looks like I'm going to be playing guitar with Fleetwood Mac. I think...

The next day we returned rested, fed, and filled with the promise of a new day. I had been practicing my four chords since we left the day before. As a folkie finger-picker, I had never played guitar with a band or played standing up. Nothing had been said to me by anybody about my new task so I approached it like another roadie chore. I set up a Fender Twin and folding chair by my tuning station and waited for further instructions. The band wandered in and rehearsals began quietly. They ran the set from the top without drama and got to *Go Your Own Way*. I picked up my guitar, sat down next to the amp and steeled myself. Stevie asked if she was playing guitar and Lindsey informed her that she was not.

"No. Raymond is," was the chilly reply.

"Congratulations," Stevie humorously offered in my direction. "I'm never speaking to you again."

"Poor Raymond," Christine fake sympathized.

John McVie delivered his best Chuck Woolery *Dating Game* introduction. "This is Raymond. He's from the Midwest. He has blue eyes and likes lobster and brandy."

With that portion of the roasting completed, Mick set the beat and Lindsey chunked his guitar as he counted us in and started the song. My contribution was shaky but not a deal breaker. It was going to take a few shows for me to find the pocket for the beginning strums. However, the straight-ahead rocking part at the end fell right into place and LB jumped on his solo with a newly discovered abandon. We kept going and going until there was nowhere left to go and surrendered to a noisy finish. For me, it was indescribable. It was such a gas to be a part of the band for that moment and such a relief that I didn't fuck it up too bad. One thing about this group, no one held back when it came to voicing their opinions about anything and I would have immediately known if there were any dissenting votes. Lindsey gave me an approving nod and I knew it was going to be OK.

After finishing the song, we moved on to the encores to finish the set. I returned to roadie mode as the evening rehearsals came to a close. In two nights I would be playing in Oakland at the Berkeley Theatre for opening night of Fleetwood Mac's Rumours World Tour but first we needed to get the truck loaded.

CHAPTER 16
DAY ON THE GREEN

The top dog committed to every detail of presenting rock shows was promoter Bill Graham. Based in San Francisco, he was a legendary producer of live music performances and put his personal stamp on everything he touched. Among his many achievements were the Fillmore's East and West, the Winterland Ballroom and a string of outdoor festivals known as the "Day on the Green." Held at the Oakland Coliseum, this series of all-day concerts began in 1973 and continued into the nineties.

In 1976 Peter Frampton was the headliner for a late spring show that featured the newly ascending Fleetwood Mac as one of the supporting acts. One year later, the Mac would fill the top spot as the *Rumours* world tour and album was picking up steam. A longtime fan and supporter of the band, Bill had put them on his stages many times. The original Fleetwood Mac with Peter Green had played both Fillmores in the late sixties and when they were forced to sue their ex-manager in 1973 over the ownership of the name "Fleetwood Mac," Bill wrote a letter to the presiding judge supporting namesakes Mick and John as the real band. The powerhouse behind Bill Graham Productions was happy about the band's recent successes and was anxious to do something special for their headline appearance.

Day On The Green Poster

Graham had a fondness for throwing in staging surprises for his favorite bands. One New Year's Eve Grateful Dead show had the theatrically-inclined promoter dressed as "Father Time" while flying in over the audience on a six-foot reefer as the clock struck midnight. For our show he had his production wizards construct a huge rainbow on the front of the eighty-foot stage that spanned the entire width of the structure. Hidden behind the audience barrier in front was a paper mache' metallic-colored cauldron on a hydraulic lift large enough to hold the five band members.

Bill was always the emcee at his shows and took great pleasure in personally introducing his performers. The plan was to have the band rise out of nowhere towards the rainbow in their pot of gold. They would then take the stage as Bill announced their arrival. The multiple logistics of ensuring perfect timing had been painstakingly worked out. A covered walkway had been built under the huge stage so the band could get to their place in front without blowing the surprise. Everyone with the production company was excited about the impending reveal.

Unfortunately, during the reset of the band's stage gear, the skies opened up and a steady downpour commenced. The deck was covered and stayed dry but the roof only extended as far as the front of the stage. The space in front where the lift was positioned was wide open and the giant gold painted bowl was already taking on water. I had returned to the dressing room to take the last guitars to the stage and walked into an animated backstage melodrama. It was showtime and Mr. Graham was pressing the group to get going. He was not going to let a spring shower spoil his finely tuned entrance. He felt the band should man/woman-up and not be so precious about getting wet for a minute or two.

This did not sit well with the female faction of the band and battle lines were being drawn. Chivalrous John McVie came to the defense of his ex-wife and invited Bill to go fuck himself. Stevie, already fighting a sore throat, cowered behind Mick and begged for protection. JC held Lindsey at bay while screaming at the irate promoter that his band would not ride up to the stage on a forklift in a downpour. I had seen Bill in action many times before and knew there were two things that he really had problems with. He was adamant about staying on schedule and he didn't do well with being told "no." Bill Graham in full rage mode was quite an event to observe. Even JC at his best/worse couldn't match the indisputable world champ. The one thing we had on our side was the seventy thousand people who had already paid and were now getting drenched waiting for their darlings.

I grabbed my guitars and left the noisy melee. Five minutes later, I see the band loading into the gold pot down below the front of the stage. It was still raining but had let up quite a bit. Bill had an umbrella in each hand—one over Chris and the other over Stevie. JC had a huge golf umbrella over the guys. As the band huddled together, they braced themselves for lift off. Promoter and manager stepped away as the machine began its noisy, holy ascension. A microphone appeared magically out of nowhere and was reeled down to the Master of Ceremonies below. He snatched it like a boxing announcer and as the lift hit stage level, brought the band on with his finest "Ladies and Gentlemen" voice.

Winner and still champion, Bill Graham.

The band was seething but finding it difficult to stay pissed with seventy thousand fans on their feet screaming their approval. It rained off and on for the whole show but the "Mac" could do no wrong. Multiple encores left the home crowd sated and filled with precious rock memories. Afterwards, all was forgiven and forgotten backstage with big hugs all around.

The "Day on the Green" concert series would continue successfully for many years with over a hundred more bands taking the stage. Fleetwood Mac would be the last act to make their entrance from a cardboard bowl on a forklift.

Rick Perea and Stevie - Day On The Green 1977

CHAPTER 17
GROWING (PAINS)

The transformation from small machine to big machine was in high gear and there was no turning back. Patrick Byrne joined our crew to handle John and Christine and let Rhyno be more flexible to stage manage. Patrick "the Beaver" Byrne was a friend of Rhyno's from Kansas City and a fellow flatlander. The Midwestern all-day dope smoking hippie was a perfect puzzle piece for our clan. The only time he wasn't smiling was when the "guy" was running late or when we were going through tunnels in the bus. The man totally shut down if we had to drive through a mountain or under a river. Europe was his worst nightmare. They're tunnel crazy over there and poor Patrick had to white knuckle it all the way through.

I was also glad to have him because Mick's newest new guy wasn't working out. He bullshitted Mick with his used car salesman smarminess while ignoring a major roadie commandment: "Thou shalt not party harder than your boss." There is a lot of live and let live on the road but everyone is responsible for recognizing their personal intake limits. Occasional lapses are forgivable but if one jeopardizes the crew's social fabric with clueless acts of self-entitlement, there will be calls for behavior modification followed by deportation. His eventual demise was hastened when he was caught going through the bunks and cleaning out the lighting guys' wallets. Time wounds all heels.

A larger production upheaval involved the dismissal of my alma mater Tycobrahe as the band's sound company. Bob Boganovich and Jim Gamble had taken their company as far as they wanted and were not interested in reinvesting to stay competitive in the touring business. Showco in Dallas and Clair Bros. of Lititz, PA were their main rivals. Both had multiple systems out with major acts but Clair was rising to the top with their innovative designs and homegrown manufacturing skills.

Gene Clair and younger brother Roy started their sound career in 1955 when their father bought them a portable P.A. system to hire out for Easter egg hunts and church functions. It was a random gift for two young teenage boys but was somehow meant to be. Their hobby turned into a business as they kept putting their rental money back into their systems. By the time they got to college, they were taking their gear on the road for Frankie Valli and The Four Seasons. In 1968, they were contracted to bring their newest system to the the Spectrum in Philadelphia for Cream's farewell tour. The success of that show caught the attention of East Coast concert promoters and they were officially in the big time.

Rurally located eighty miles from Philadelphia in the rolling hills of Amish country, their first shop was in a barn. They employed talent locally and tapped into the nearby colleges for recruits, often seeking out sturdy and determined student wrestlers. In a practice that could have only existed in an era before human resources departments, new job applicants were encouraged to grapple in a best two out of three with ex-wrestlers, Roy and Gene. Their top electronics engineers came out of the same schools as well and the conservative company moved steadily to the top of their field. In 1974, their newest design was the S4 speaker cabinet and became the industry standard for twenty years until the arrival of line array systems. Four feet wide and four feet high, the black four-way cabinets were designed to lock together and hang from the ceiling in whatever array was appropriate for the stage and arena size. It was large, powerful, and impressive. Fleetwood Mac would never be not loud enough again.

Along with a new sound company came a new gang of sound guys. Acerbic Trip Khalif, dapper Gene Pelland, enlightened Chuck Hull and beloved Jim DeVenney were the "A-Team" sent out to capture the audio hearts of a not easily impressed Fleetwood Mac. It took one show and it was game on. Trip was the system head and spent all day setting up and dialing in the system so Richard Dashut could arrive with the band and start mixing. An intelligent and skilled engineer, Trip was also a mouthy, wise ass know-it-all. I liked him right away. I was sorry to see my old friends go but the new guys brought fresh firepower to the crew. Almost immediately, I was confronted by Trip about my gig as sideman on *Go Your Own Way.* He didn't understand why I was sitting offstage hiding behind a guitar amplifier. I had been playing the acoustic guitar part for six months and had found a suitable groove. Staying under the radar was part of the gig. Trip appointed himself my manager and challenged me to grow a pair. His new mission was to not shut up until I came out of the wings and joined in with the rest of the band.

Trip, Me and the Beav

My biggest problem with this transition was not performance anxiety but my lack of experience playing guitar standing up. My entire

117

history of playing since I first picked up a 6 string had been done sitting down and my arms and hands had to get retrained to strum from a new angle. It took a week of practicing to get comfortable. I was ready to try it out at sound check but Trip insisted I wait till showtime for maximum impact. That night I walked on stage next to Lindsey and waited for him to notice my upgraded placement. He gave me a look that seemed to ask "What the fuck are you doing here?" After the initial shock wore off he acknowledged my new position with a tight smile. The rest of the band welcomed me warmly and I proceeded to bang out my part with a new passion and conviction. I never sat on the side of the stage again. It was the right thing to do even if it was Trip's idea.

An even more substantial and positive shake-up in my life also took place on this tour. The beautiful and enthusiastic Christie Alsbury was traveling with the band as Stevie and Christine's makeup artist. Christie was a friend of Stevie's and had been around our scene for a couple of years. There was no question that she was out of my league and I had never thought a girl like her would be looking at me. Perhaps my new gig as rock and roll guitar player was starting to pay off. We enjoyed the summer together but the insanity of a Fleetwood Mac tour was not conducive to nurturing extended relationships. Almost thirty years later at a Fleetwood Mac rehearsal, we were steered towards each other by mutual friend Margi Kent and had the good sense to fall in love again. This time it was for keeps as we married in October 2003 and have been happily taking care of each other since. A rare Fleetwood Mac love story with a happy ending. It was meant to be.

Christie & Stevie 1977

We were now up to three semi trucks of equipment. Besides tons more lighting and the expanded sound system, there was all the rigging required to hang everything from above. We were growing up big time. Rhyno was keeping up with the accumulating production demands but was starting to get overwhelmed. On a hot sticky set-up day in Milwaukee at a baseball stadium, a liquored-up John McVie decided to test the patience of his longtime crew chief. The normally kind-hearted bass player was not doing well with his divorce from Christine and his vodka-fueled alter ego Mr. Hyde was gearing up for another tedious round of "Victim of the Day." This had unfortunately become McVie's new way to kill time and he decided to spend this particular afternoon dogging an already stressed-out Rhyno.

It was a simple game—keep pushing your target's buttons until a bull's-eye is scored. Once John smelled blood, he was relentless until the kill. He stalked his prey *du jour all* over the backstage area until he was cornered and pushed to his limits. I was literally hanging by both hands off of the bicep of Rhyno's cocked right arm to stop him from leveling the oblivious bass player. When JC walked in on me wrestling my buddy off of the toasted rock star, McVie's ass holiness was derailed and he was sent back to his hotel room.

★ ★ ★

In the fall of 1977, we were booked for six weeks of shows in Australia and Japan. It was decided that we would take our new P.A. with us and not be subjected to whatever local rentals awaited us. A stretch DC-8 allegedly acquired from a CIA front company, was appropriated to handle the transportation of sound and band gear. Set up for hauling cargo, the stretch configuration was longer than the standard model and accommodated fifteen pallets that got loaded and secured on the ground before being popped into the hold. The final deck, pallet sixteen, sat in the rear with a couple dozen seats screwed to the floor. This is how the crew traveled to Australia, Japan, Hawaii, and home. There was a bathroom, a couple of ice chests, and a microwave for our traveling comfort. The oven was used only once as it was found to interfere with the aircraft's tail flaps when reheating food. With no movies or music channels, we were left to our own devices for passing the time on the eighteen-hour flight from LAX to Sydney. Fortunately, lighting man Dave Richanbach's back problems qualified him for a generous allotment of Valium. His pills, and the plane's stash of Vodka, provided many hours of painless slumber for the econo travelers. After we made it to Sydney to begin our tour, a plan was hatched to recoup our money for the transport plane.

Since the DC-8 was sitting idle while we did our shows, an offer was taken to sublease the aircraft to a company transporting livestock. The tour made a profit on the deal but the last half of our trip was considerably smellier. After a few weeks "Down Under" we moved onto

Japan and finished in Hawaii on the island of Maui. The local airstrip at Kahului was an international airport and routinely handled jet traffic, but they had never seen a plane our size. Our craft's maxed-out length and load tested their limits as we used every foot of runway from touchdown to full stop. We had to be towed backwards for a few hundred feet before we reached a place on the tarmac where we could disembark. The tallest set of rolling stairs available was wheeled out to us and placed at the door at the rear of the plane. The top step was five feet below the bottom of the door frame and we all had to shimmy out on our stomachs to reach the stairs. Our last show of the tour was at the Lahaina Tennis Courts.

Rumours Touring Party 1977

In a gesture of goodwill, I was presented with a grocery bag full of premium Maui homegrown from Lindsey. It was stuffed full with a dozen stalks of buds the size of my arm. The next day we boarded the DC-8 one last time for our flight home and I broke out the herbal tour bonus to divvy up amongst my crew mates. As spliffs began to circulate on pallet sixteen, we were finally successful in overpowering the earthy bouquet of bovine urine and feces.

The *Rumours* album was #1 on the Billboard charts for thirty-one weeks and went on to win a Grammy for album of the year. It was selling a million copies a month with no sign of slowing down. We sold out every show in every town we played. Two years earlier when the band was in court fighting their old manager, Clifford, and living gig to gig on their box office take, there was not a real manager in the world that would touch them. Everything we had achieved to this point had been accomplished in-house and it was difficult to make an argument for bringing in a highly paid outside opinion. Why give fifteen percent to somebody no one was going to listen to? And so, Seedy Management, the band's DYI management company with Mick and John at the helm, continued to oversee the game winning strategies that had become the Fleetwood Mac way. Balancing their success with a sense of humor, Mick and John took out a full-page ad in Billboard with a picture of the pair entering a Hollywood Blvd. pawn shop in trench coats with the band's gold records under their arms. This had been an incredibly successful year and everyone was working on ways to coexist in a mutually respectful fashion. As new members of the "big machine" club, the band was obliged to continue marching forward in the style that got them there. It was time to begin working on a new album and no expense was to be spared paying tribute to the all powerful God of Recording.

CHAPTER 18
TUSK ALBUM

In February 1978, we began pre-production for the next album. A house on Mulholland Drive above Studio City was rented for a couple months of writing and inspiration seeking. It was a modestly furnished ranch home with bedrooms on opposite ends and a good size combo living room/dining room in the middle. There was a small backyard with a pool and jacuzzi that had a sweeping view of the San Fernando Valley. The entire property sat on a finger of land that stood by itself away from neighbors. We were secluded, isolated, and secure. Rhyno was on tour with Bob Welch so I stayed in town to run the rehearsals. I cleared out the living room and set up a performance area with an ample selection of band gear. After putting together a little monitor system for vocals, we were good to go. After claiming the bedroom farthest from the action, I settled in for nine weeks of rehearsal and medium level mayhem.

The first couple of weeks started gung ho and probably produced the bulk of anything musically useful for the studio. About the time Mick took over the bedroom on the other side of the house is when the project turned away from album prep and moved towards Mick's midnight clubhouse of music and storytelling. It became the site of many late-night jams with various guitar bearing creatures strolling in, and many hours later crawling out. The last significant blowout featured Lindsey, Christine, and John with Neil Young and Ron Wood. It was a spirited and lengthy festival and marked the unofficial beginning of Mick's decade-long never-ending party.

* * *

The Village Recorder in Santa Monica would be the sight of our next recording adventure, but first a new studio needed to be built. Erected in the 1920's as a Masonic Temple, the ornate and unique building that housed The Village was purchased in 1968 by Geordie Hormel, heir to the Hormel meatpacking dynasty. Geordie had stumbled into the TV music business in L.A. in the 1950's. An unusable recording of his first attempt at writing orchestral scores ended up in the hands of television producers needing low budget background music for shows like *Lassie and Leave it to Beaver.* The novice composer's unsuccessful outing with serious music turned into broadcasting gold. At one point, Geordie's cue music was on half of the TV shows being produced. Between his scoring money and profits from Spam, Geordie made his way into the recording business and built The Village Recorder.

The original facility housed two studios and was famous for both it's architectural eccentricities as well as sonic superiority. In the early seventies it was a prime destination for artists with sophisticated recording tastes. When Geordie was approached by Ken Caillat and the band to block out a year of studio time for their next project, he responded by offering to build them their own studio in an adjacent part of his building. A million dollars later, Studio D was designed, built, and handed over to Fleetwood Mac for their creative and recording needs. It was a masterpiece and combined a comfortable space with technical elegance. Besides a large recording area and a control room big enough for the engineers and band, there were lounges, a kitchen, and ample storage space. All of this was completely private and accessible only through a single door that opened out to the street. It was the ultimate recording play space and suited the Fleetwood Mac work ethic perfectly.

Musically, this project was the most pure reflection of the band's creative talents and their nonstop successes inspired them to take the recording process as far as they could imagine. The Studio D sessions produced some of the most atmospheric and vibe-driven tracks the band has ever recorded. It is essential Fleetwood Mac listening. This would be the last time that Fleetwood Mac as a band would be the sole recipient of everyone's combined talents, tunes, and commitment.

Studio D Main Lounge

Working in the studio was very much the opposite of touring and if you weren't involved in the hands-on participation of the daily tasks, time could move very slow. Being on the road was all about defined goals and challenges that delivered daily gratification. There was a beginning, middle, and end to every day. No matter what, showtime was at eight and a few hours later, the door on the last truck would be closed and locked. Working methodically with like-minded craftsmen was more my cup of tea.

The recording process for Fleetwood Mac was all about avoiding most types of structure. There was a defined series of record making events that would eventually be completed, but the path there was casually vague. Any planning interpreted as counter to creativity was eyed with suspicion. Watching this slow motion movie from the wings could be a bit mind numbing but it was a necessary evil. You don't go on tour until you make a record. The better the record, the bigger the tour. After finishing the Bob Welch tour, Rhyno returned to Kansas City while the band continued their recording marathon. To bide some time and pay some bills, my #1 roadie began working in the telecommunications industry in his hometown. By the time we finished the double album, Rhyno had recalibrated his priorities and decided to stay home.

My years outlasting all the other crew guys had afforded me a working knowledge of every piece of gear the band possessed. Since a major goal of this recording project was access to all options at all times, I always had something to do. Everything we owned was brought to the Village and set up in the huge recording side of the studio. Patrick had come out from Missouri to give me a hand and Greg Thomason from the touring security force helped with food, driving, and comic relief. Everyone in the band wanted to try stuff we didn't own so I was always searching for and acquiring unique sound and music making devices. A lot of my time was spent figuring out how to make one of a kind prototypes work in a way that someone could actually play and hopefully record with.

I built a fully stocked workshop in the storage room where our collection of eighty guitars and basses was kept. On hand was a staggering inventory of various makes, gauges, and styles of guitar strings. There were crates of spare tubes for our guitar amps as well as all of my tools, files, clamps, and test gear. I needed every resource available to meet the daily challenge of "stump the roadie" from Lindsey, Richard, and Ken.

Mick was a passionate seeker of drum related oddities and a colorful collection of people would randomly show up at the studio with offerings for the pope of percussion. Our drummer had a gift for engaging the cosmic wanderers of the world, and one of my tasks was to graciously initiate an exit when guests had outstayed their welcome. The rest of the band would let me know when it was time to reclaim their privacy so I would trade a beer for a business card and help the reluctant visitor find the parking lot.

Lindsey, Mick & John Studio D Control Room

In the spirit of innovation and discovery, Fleetwood came up with an idea that was one of the first attempts at percussion sampling. After filming a murder movie spoof with Richard and LB called *The Harmonica Killer* in the bowels of the former Masonic Temple, Mick wondered aloud about the percussive possibilities of human bodies meeting unfortunate circumstances. Dashut, a shameless Mick enabler, joined in and continued the morbid discussion on various scenarios of demise and what type of audio might be generated. The conversation progressed with Mick and Richard deciding we should conduct experiments of our own.

While I drove over to the nearby Ralph's market to purchase cuts of raw meat, Hernan, our second engineer, ran some microphones outside to the sidewalk by our door. When I returned, we hiked up to the roof and proceeded to record the sound made by chunks of animal parts hitting the pavement from three stories up. We didn't get to really get into it as the local police station was changing shifts and the constant traffic of patrol cars cruising by put a damper on our enthusiasm. When we listened back to what was captured on tape, it was decided to shelve the project until larger cuts, preferably whole sides of beef, could be secured.

We never revisited meat sampling but Mick did manage to over-dub a percussion part on the song *Tusk* using a spatula to slap a leg of lamb. There was one other significant food related incident during the recording, but this involved cooked proteins instead of raw. An offer of one million dollars was extended to the band from McDonald's in exchange for an original tune extolling the virtues of the Big Mac. For reasons too numerous to count, the offer was declined.

The ambitious double album was finished in the summer of 1979. A year-long world tour was scheduled to start in the fall following a month of rehearsals. We acquired our own stage that we would carry with us and a vast collection of bigger, better, brighter lights. All this required more trucks, more crew and more buses for the added bodies. The size of the machine had expanded once again and Mick's imagination kept pace.

TUSK TOUR
OCTOBER 1979

26	POCATELLA IDAHO	MINI DOME IDAHO ST UNIVERSITY
27	OGDEN UTAH	DEE EVENTS CENTER
28	SALT LAKE CITY UTAH	SALT PALACE ARENA
29		
30		
31	DENVER C0LORADO	MCNICHOLS ARENA

NOVEMBER 1979

01	DENVER COLORADO	MCNICHOLS ARENA
02	ALBUQUERQUE NEW MEXICO	TINGLEY COLISEUM
03		
04		
05	ST. LOUIS MISSOURI	CHECKERDOME
06	ST. LOUIS MISSOURI	CHECKERDOME
07	CINCINNATI OHIO	RIVERFRONT STADIUM
08		
09		
10	NEW HAVEN CONNECTICUT	NEW HAVEN COLISEUM
11	HEMPSTEAD LONG ISLAND NY	NASSAU COLISEUM
12	HEMPSTEAD LONG ISLAND NY	NASSAU COLISEUM
13		
14		
15	NEW YORK NEW YORK	MADISON SQUARE GARDEN
16	NEW YORK NEW YORK	MADISON SQUARE GARDEN
17	BOSTON MASSACHUSETTS	BOSTON GARDENS
18		
19		
20	ROCHESTER NEW YORK	WAR MEMORIAL STADIUM
21	PHILADELPHIA PENNSYLVANIA	THE SPECTRUM

22 PROVIDENCE RHODE ISLAND   CIVIC CENTER
23
24
25 LARGO MARYLAND   CAPITAL CENTER
26 PITTSBURGH PENNSYLVANIA   CIVIC ARENA
27
28
29 ANN ARBOR MICHIGAN   CHRYSLER ARENA
30 CHAMPAIGN ILLINOIS   UNIVERSITY OF ILLINOIS

DECEMBER 1979

01 CEDAR FALLS IOWA   UNI DOME
02
03
04 LOS ANGELES CALIFORNIA   THE FORUM
05 LOS ANGELES CALIFORNIA   THE FORUM
06 LOS ANGELES CALIFORNIA   THE FORUM
07
08
09 SAN DIEGO CALIFORNIA   SPORTS ARENA
10 LOS ANGELES CALIFORNIA   THE FORUM
11 LOS ANGELES CALIFORNIA   THE FORUM
12
13
14 SAN FRANCISCO CALIFORNIA   COW PALACE
15 SAN FRANCISCO CALIFORNIA   COW PALACE
16 SAN FRANCISCO CALIFORNIA   COW PALACE

FEBRUARY 1980

03 TOKYO JAPAN   THE BUDOKAN
04 TOKYO JAPAN   THE BUDOKAN
05 TOKYO JAPAN   THE BUDOKAN
06
07

08	KYOTO JAPAN	THE KAIKAN
09	GIFU JAPAN	THE SHIMAN KAIKAN
10	SAPPORO JAPAN	KUSEINENKIN HALL
11		
12		
13	YOKOHAMA JAPAN	KENMIN HALL
14	SENDAI HALL	SPORTS HALL
15		
16	OSAKA JAPAN	FESTIVAL HALL
17	OSAKA JAPAN	FESTIVAL HALL
18		
19		
20		
21	PERTH AUSTRALIA	ENTERTAINMENT CENTER
22	PERTH AUSTRALIA	ENTERTAINMENT CENTER
23		
24		
25	ADELAIDE AUSTRALIA	TENNIS STADIUM
26		
27	SYDNEY AUSTRALIA	HORDEN PAVILLION
28	SYDNEY AUSTRALIA	HORDEN PAVILLION

MARCH 1980

01	MELBOURNE AUSTRALIA	FESTIVAL HALL
02	MELBOURNE AUSTRALIA	FESTIVAL HALL
03	MELBOURNE AUSTRALIA	FESTIVAL HALL
04		
05		
06	BRISBANE AUSTRALIA	FESTIVAL HALL
07	BRISBANE AUSTRALIA	FESTIVAL HALL
08	BRISBANE AUSTRALIA	FESTIVAL HALL
09		
10		
11	MELBOURNE AUSTRALIA	FESTIVAL HALL

12	MELBOURNE AUSTRALIA	FESTIVAL HALL
13		
14		
15	SYDNEY AUSTRALIA	HORDEN PAVILLION
16	SYDNEY AUSTRALIA	HORDEN PAVILLION
17	SYDNEY AUSTRALIA	HORDEN PAVILLION
18		
19		
20	WELLINGTON NEW ZEALAND	ATHLETIC PARK
21		
22	AUCKLAND NEW ZEALAND	
23		
24		
25		
26		
27	HONOLULU HAWAII	BLAISDELL ARENA
28	HONOLULU HAWAII	BLAISDELL ARENA
29	HONOLULU HAWAII	BLAISDELL ARENA

APRIL 1980

30	PORTLAND OREGON	PORTLAND COLISEUM

MAY 1980

01	SEATTLE WASHINGTON	EDMUNSON PAVILLION
02	VANCOUVER CANADA	PNE COLISEUM
03		
04		
05	EDMONTON CANADA	EDMONTON COLISEUM
06	EDMONTON CANADA	EDMONTON COLISEUM
07		
08		
09	MINNEAPOLIS MINNESOTA	MET CENTER
10	MINNEAPOLIS MINNESOTA	MET CENTER
11	MADISON WISCONSIN	DANE COUNTY ARENA

12
13
14 CHICAGO ILLINOIS   ROSEMONT HORIZON
15 CHICAGO ILLINOIS   ROSEMONT HORIZON
16 INDIANAPOLIS INDIANA   MARKET SQUARE ARENA
17
18
19 BUFFALO NEW YORK   MUNICIPAL AUDITORIUM
20 RICHFIELD OHIO   RICHFIELD COLISEUM
21 RICHFIELD OHIO   RICHFIELD COLISEUM
22
23 DETROIT MICHIGAN   JOE LOUIS ARENA
24 DETROIT MICHIGAN   JOE LOUIS ARENA

JUNE 1980

01 MUNICH GERMANY   OLYMPIC STADIUM
02
03 BREMEN GERMANY   STADTHALLE
04 COLOGNE GERMANY   SPORTSHALLE
05 DORTMUND GERMANY   WESTFALENHALLE
06
07
08 FRANKFURT GERMANY   BETZENBURG STADIUM
09 ZURICH SWITZERLAND   HALLENSTADION
10
11
12 BRUSSELS BELGIUM   FOREST NATIONAL
13 ROTTERDAM HOLLAND   THE AHOY
14 PARIS FRANCE   PALAIS DE SPORT
15
16 STAFFORD ENGLAND   BINGLEY HALL
17 STAFFORD ENGLAND   BINGLEY HALL
18
19

20	LONDON ENGLAND	WEMBLEY ARENA
21	LONDON ENGLAND	WEMBLEY ARENA
22	LONDON ENGLAND	WEMBLEY ARENA
23		
24		
25	LONDON ENGLAND	WEMBLEY ARENA
26	LONDON ENGLAND	WEMBLEY ARENA
27	LONDON ENGLAND	WEMBLEY ARENA

AUGUST 1980

05	LAKELAND FLORIDA	LAKELAND CIVIC CENTER
06	MIAMI FLORIDA	HOLLYWOOD SPORTATORIUM
07		
08	ATLANTA GEORGIA	THE OMNI
09		
10		
11	MOBILE ALABAMA	MOBILE AUDITORIUM
12	BIRMINGHAM ALABAMA	JEFFERSON CIVIC CENTER
13	BATON ROUGE	CENTROPLEX
14		
15		
16	DALLAS TEXAS	REUNION ARENA
17	SAN ANTONIO TEXAS	CONVENTION CENTER ARENA
18	HOUSTON TEXAS	THE SUMMIT
19		
20		
21	OMAHA NEBRASKA	OMAHA CIVIC CENTER
22	OKLAHOMA CITY OKLAHOMA	MYRIAD CONVENTION CENTER
23	WICHITA KANSAS	KANSAS COLISEUM
24	KANSAS CITY KANSAS	KEMPER ARENA

25
26
27 LAS CRUCES NEW MEXICO   PAN AMERICAN CENTER
28 TUCSON ARIZONA   MCHALE CENTER
29 TEMPE ARIZONA   COMPTON TERRACE

SEPTEMBER 1980
01 HOLLYWOOD CALIFORNIA   HOLLYWOOD BOWL

CHAPTER 19
TUSK TOUR

When we started recording at The Village, studio owner Geordie made a rare appearance early in the project to share with us his knowledge of a scientific phenomenon based on Russian research from the 1930's. Looking and sounding like a visiting professor, he explained to us the physics of positive and negative ions. We learned that negative ions are oxygen atoms charged with an extra electron. They are created in nature by the combined effects of water, air, and sunlight. Negatively charged ions are mostly found in natural places and particularly around moving water or after a thunderstorm. The taste in the air and feeling you get at the beach, near a waterfall, or after a storm is the result of your body being saturated in the benefits of negative ions. In high enough concentrations, negative ions clear the air of mold spores, pollen, odors, cigarette smoke, bacteria, viruses, and other nasty airborne particles. Environments filled with electronic equipment and forced air climate control—like recording studios—are loaded with unwanted positively ionized air. Prolonged exposure to positive ions can produce headaches, nasal obstruction, dryness of throat and dizziness.

After completing his dissertation, Geordie faced little resistance convincing the band to accept the presence of the innocuous black box in the corner of the studio silently bathing the tainted atmosphere with restorative good ions. The only thing ironically not factored in was the abundance of brandy, blow, and weed already being utilized to promote all kinds of states of perceived wellbeing. One has to question the effectiveness of a lowly single ion generator against these proven less subtle methods of mood maintenance.

Mick was the band's most passionate believer in the powers of negative ion generation and wanted to take the energy enhancing qualities out of the studio and on the road. He found a guy who had built a system powerful enough to cover a thousand-square-foot area, roughly the size of the performance area of our new stage. The hipster scientists spent one of our rehearsal dark days suspending over a hundred microphone-sized cylinders from the lighting truss above the heads of the band. Everybody showed up early the next day and lounged on the stage like they were at the beach.

There were varying degrees of acceptance with John providing the loudest dissenting vote. Chris and Stevie were amused and offered the most optimism in support of Mick. Lindsey maintained a fake neutrality and kept reaching up to touch the sensor that was hanging directly above his head. He would get a static electricity snap every time he made contact and kept messing with it until it became a group distraction. When the ion guru in charge of the immense system asked Lindsey to stop touching his stuff it was pretty much game over. He missed completely that this was LB's way of saying get that shit out of here. The system was shut down for the rest of the night and was taken down before we came back the next day.

These rehearsals were "closed" but anyone invited by a band member was granted access and the Fleetwood Mac movable feast was in high gear. There was a full bar, and every night band and crew enjoyed a catered sit-down meal. Among the friends and family attending were purveyors of specialty items attractive to the seventies rock community. The jewelers brought handmade chains of pure gold and silver. The guitar collectors offered everything from vintage D'Angelico New Yorkers to Gretsch White Falcons. The absolute most over the top presentation came from a specialty automobile broker and involved a matching pair of 1955 Mercedes 300SL gull-wing race cars. No takers on that one.

The nerd roadie in me was stoked that our show had attained big machine status. With Chris Lamb as production manager and rigger Jim Barnes in charge of hanging everything from the rafters, all the pieces were in place. Jeff Sova, the Shah of Jazz, was installed as our first legit keyboard specialist and took care of everything in Christine's world. Our long search for a drum roadie with the right skills and temperament had come to an end. From Cleveland, we brought in Tony Todaro, a good Italian boy with a warm heart, strong constitution, and total devotion to Mick's wellbeing. We still had Patrick looking after John and I kept everything sorted out for Lindsey as well as managing the stage.

For the first time all of our onstage bases were covered. My vision of functionality and organization of the band's gear had finally been realized. All of the stage hardware had been upgraded and made bulletproof. We carried spares for all of the the critical electronics and every box of gear had been numbered and labeled with stage directions for the local crews. I inventoried and valued every thing we owned for the accountant's insurance rider. Serial numbers, weights, and dimensions of each road case were documented for international freight carnets. Through attrition, I had inadvertently become the voice of reason and responsible adult of the band crew. My rules for survival were simple. Pay attention, practice good hygiene, and always be ready with a "Plan B".

My extra credit assignment playing guitar on stage was the original rock and roll fantasy camp. Thanks to my self-appointed manager, Trip Khalaf, I had successfully moved from playing in darkness in the wings to being bathed by a spotlight on stage with my own monitor. *Go Your Own Way* was always the last song in the set before encores. Every night at the appointed time I would chug a cold Heineken and stroll over to Lindsey with my Ovation steel string. LB would coax me to mildly jam with him as he chunked out some time before starting the song. I would keep it going until I got the nod and off we would go.

The next five minutes would transport me into the ultimate rock vortex. Playing on one of the biggest songs in the band's catalog with an entire arena of fans on their feet never got old. As Lindsey would begin to dig into his solo, I would step back to the drums and lock in with Mick and John all the way to the big finish. There would be just enough time for me take my guitar off and grab Lindsey's from him as the band walked offstage.

Raysworld

Like Superman back to Clark Kent, I would instantly return to roadie and start tuning guitars for the encore. All of my mates on the road crew found this amusing and graciously granted me my fantasy fun time. Jim DeVenney would keep my monitors cranked and Curry would always cue a SuperTrooper to keep me drenched in lumens. As long I still called the truck pack after the show, my boys kindly allowed me my brief moment of rock star glory.

Every night I played was a gas, but my favorite memory comes from the night a couple of Rolling Stones appeared at a gig. We were playing the first of two sold-out nights in Madison Square Garden when halfway through the set, Keith Richards and Ron Wood appear beside me at my work area beside the stage. I knew Woody from his visits to our band house on Mulholland and made some room for the pair. I made sure their drinks were topped off and got back to work. They were entertaining guests and had a great time checking out all the gear while taking in the show. Toward the end of the set, I strapped my Ovation on to check the tuning and prepare for my entrance. At first, Keith didn't seem to care much about the plastic bowl of a guitar around my neck until two things caught his eye. First, it had a capo high on the eighth fret and secondly, it only had five strings. We had taken the low "E" string off because the root note of the chords I was playing was on the fifth string and the sixth wasn't needed.

Keith was famous among guitarists for playing in open tunings that chucked the superfluous low string as well. He was even more amused when I kept the guitar on and stepped around the pair to climb the steps and take my place on stage. It was an over the top NYC night at the Garden and *Go Your Own Way* didn't disappoint. Once again, I happily rode the band's coattails for my five minutes of personal rock bliss.

When the song finished I returned to my tuning station and noticed my two guests had disappeared. Twenty minutes later, the band finished their encores and left the stage for the last time. Since there was another show at the Garden the next night, the crew didn't have a lot to do. I locked up my guitars and headed to the dressing room for a beverage. I was drinking a beer with Lindsey when Keith appears from behind me, throws his arm around my shoulders and bestows upon me with classic Keith Richards' incoherence: "That was fuckin' great, man!" Woody hugged me from the other side and offered his own drunken words of admiration. For a brief, priceless moment I was the center of attention between the two Rolling Stones guitar players. Sensing it was time to redirect the focus back on my boss, I shared the story of LB listening to *Street Fighting Man* at the Record Plant bunk house in Mill Valley and getting the idea for the drums on his song. This pleased the two guitarists greatly and the conversation veered back to Charlie Watts and old Stones records. The dressing room was suddenly filled with crew guys not used to having free time after a show so I excused myself and melted into their crowd.

★ ★ ★

In December, we were booked for three nights at the Forum in Los Angeles. The title song of the new album, *Tusk,* featured the USC Trojan Marching Band. Recorded at Dodger Stadium on the Wally Heider mobile recording truck, the one hundred and twelve-piece ensemble set a record for the most musicians performing on a single and was a shining example of how over the top the recording of the album had become. On tour, keyboard tech Jeff Sova would play the marching band part on a synthesizer offstage and was a convincing fill in. For the Mac's California homecoming, the real USC band was brought to the Forum and installed behind floor to ceiling curtains at the rear of the stage. When we got to *Tusk* in the set and the marching band's musical entry point, the curtains dropped from the ceiling revealing all 112 collegiate players. After a full round of their majestic arrangement, the

Trojan ensemble split up and marched down the aisles to the rear of the Fabulous Forum and back. It was an LA worthy presentation.

A somewhat less effective bonus element was scratched after the first night's show due to lack of execution and near asphyxiation. Traditionally, there was always a twenty-five to thirty-minute intermission between our opening act and Fleetwood Mac's performance. We would peel off the first band's gear and recheck the Mac inputs while music was played over the P.A.

To spice up the interval, Mick found an escape artist to perform before the band's entrance. A large floor safe was carried to the deck by a squadron of union hands and set in the center down front. The house lights went out and the "Great Ronzoni" strolled to the pool of light focused on the middle of the stage. He introduced himself and shared with the audience his promise to dazzle them with his first time-ever presentation of releasing himself from multiple implements of bondage in front of a live audience. After strapping into a straightjacket and clicking on handcuffs, Ronzoni was locked into the safe while the rest of us looked on. Five minutes, eight minutes, ten minutes passed and an understandable mood of confusion began to fill the arena.

I was standing on the left side of the stage with Leo Rossi, one of our lighting regulars, when tour manager John Courage appeared and began to take stock of the debacle tainting his band's stage. It had now been fifteen minutes of seventeen thousand vibrating rock fans all staring at the black box bathed in white light. We had surpassed the absurdity point ten minutes previous and the band was now standing offstage ready to get their show on.

JC sent promoter Bill Reed out to a microphone to pretend that this was all a big joke while the stage hands returned to lug the safe to the back of the stage and onto a waiting forklift. While Courage introduced the band to their grateful fans and Fleetwood Mac music filled the room, a small army of backstage personnel pried open the trap door of the prop safe. Inside they found an unconscious and less than "great" Ronzoni. A few lungfuls of Inglewood oxygen and some smelling salts revived the perplexed performer and the house medics returned to their post. Another ambitious Fleetwood Mac endeavor that made it to the list of things to never do again.

Leo Rossi, John and Christine

A week later, we finished up the year in the Bay area where the "Colonel" would be the recipient of the ultimate road payback. Every rock tour with any credibility is filled with practical jokes and jokers and JC was no stranger to these events. He was a primary instigator and a leader in his field. Courage didn't share much about his youth but I did know that after spending a summer as a teen "modifying" live chickens for "processing", he developed a deep and abiding loathing of of all things poultry. This rare crack in his armor would later resurface as the theme of a covert mission implemented by promoter Don Fox. While the band and JC were at the gig at the Cow Palace in nearby Daly City, Don and partner Ray Compton orchestrated a barn yard make over in Courage's room at the elegant St. Francis Hotel, the group's lodgings for the three night stand of shows. Bales of straw, generous helpings of chicken feed and ashtrays filled with cognac were among the accommodations provided for the two dozen VIP yard birds lucky enough to be attending their first and only rock and roll road rave.

When the band returned eight hours later after finishing the evening's show, JC opened the door to his room and walked in to find a holy mess of ungodly proportions. After 10 minutes of inconsolable outrage, he eventually acknowledged that he had been outplayed and conceded temporary victory to his tormentors. The second wave of the party soon kicked in as everybody in the entourage showed up to get a look at the only suite at the St. Francis decorated by Future Farmers of America. Sometime around seven in the morning when the upper crust of the Golden Gate city began to gather in the lobby of the city's most prestigious hotel to start their day, the elevator doors opened next to the front desk and twenty four non registered feathered guests strolled out, ready to call it a night. Many thousands of dollars quickly found their way to the manager's office in an effort to smooth things over. This gesture was enough to fend off any dealings with the authorities but wasn't effective in preventing the banning of Fleetwood Mac from ever stepping foot again in the world famous five star St. Francis Hotel.

The *Tusk* tour picked up again in February with stops in Japan, Australia, the U.S., Europe and back to the States in the summer. We finished on September 1st at the Hollywood Bowl in Los Angeles. Success did not suck.

Hollywood Bowl

It was a fine pure feeling to be on top. One was sure that the lights shone upon fair ladies and brave men. That pianos dripped the right notes and that the young lips singing them spoke with happy hearts. All these beautiful faces, for instance, must be absolutely happy.

The Last Kiss
F. Scott Fitzgerald

CHAPTER 20
ROADIE OF THE YEAR

Many industries have their own trade publications that cater to the people doing business in that specific field. Hotel owners print their own magazine with facts and figures showing how competitors are faring in shared markets. Mortuary Monthly covers the top ten bargain casket choices. In the seventies, as rock bands were rolling into arenas across the country, the promoters putting up the money for these shows had their own weekly periodical. *Performance* magazine dealt solely with the box office results of every band on tour. It would list each act's tour dates, where they played, what the venue's capacity was and how many seats were actually sold. They reported the ticket prices and how much money each show made. This was no nonsense financial nuts and bolts and a valuable cog in the gears of all big rock machines and the promoters making a nice living off of them.

Once a year *Performance* would conduct an industry poll based on promoters' experiences with the touring acts they had worked with the previous twelve months. The topics of prime interest focused on the financial successes of the top bands and the venues and markets they did business in. There were also categories for all the related vendors in the field. They voted on best lighting, sound, staging, trucking, merchandising, and so on. Included in the list was "Roadie of the Year."

In early 1980, I got a message from our business office, Penguin Promotions, that a writer for *Performance* would like to talk to me. I had been interviewed by music magazines about the band's stage equipment before and assumed this was what he wanted to talk about.

When I returned the call, I was brought up to speed about their current yearly roundup poll. He said every top promoter in the country was a big fan of mine and I had swept the voting in the "Best Roadie" category. I was complimented on my professionalism and steady, calm demeanor. Although nice to hear, I had never been openly accused of any of those traits in the ball-busting world of road crews. He also asked me about my guitar racks. He had seen one and thought they were brilliant. I confirmed the racks were my design and had been building them for four years. The writer then inquired about my schedule for May. When I told him we were in the middle of a year-long tour and that I would be in Europe at that time, he seemed disappointed.

A movie about rock bands called "Roadie" starring Meatloaf was being released and the film's PR guys wanted to connect the premiere with the announcement of the magazine's real roadie award. He was hoping I could attend the opening and be a part of the publicity package. I restated my scheduling conflict and respectfully declined the offer to help them legitimize their film. It would have been tough for me to get into participating in this even if I was in the country. I was still trying to wrap my head around the concept of a roadie award and knew I would be suffering endless digs from my peers when this got out.

Months passed and the phone call from *Performance* magazine had long been forgotten when the Penguin office sent me the most recent edition of the trade paper. On the cover was a picture from the premier of the movie "Roadie." There was Meatloaf, a *Performance* magazine executive, and a roadie-looking guy standing uncomfortably on the end.

Here's the beginning of the reprinted article that went with the cover:

"Mike Sherrill, stage manager for Styx, finished in a tie with Ray Lindsay, Fleetwood Mac's guitar roadie extraordinaire, for this year's *Performance* Readers Poll 'Roadie of the Year Award.' *Performance* delayed the announcement of our winners in this category so that our awards could be presented at a special prerelease screening of the United Artists' film *Roadie*. Ray, however, was on tour in Germany with Fleetwood Mac and missed this particular party. Below, our New York Bureau Chief, Jim Cowen, brings us up to date with the latest in a series of interviews with our behind-the-scenes Award Winners. We will have a similar interview with co-winner, Ray Lindsay, later in the summer during Fleetwood Mac's U.S. tour."

Performance Cover

1979 Readers Poll Award Winner

"Roadie of the Year"
Mike Sherrill

Mike Sherrill, stage manager for Styx, finished in a tie with Ray Lindsay, Fleetwood Mac's guitar roadie extraordinaire, for this year's PERFORMANCE Readers Poll Roadie of the Year Award. PERFORMANCE delayed the announcement of our winners in this category so that our awards could be presented at a special pre-release screening of the United Artists' film "Roadie". Ray, however, was on tour in Germany with Fleetwood Mac and missed this particular party. Below, our New York Bureau Chief, Jim Cowen, brings us up to date with the latest in a series of interviews with our behind-the-scenes Award Winners. We will have a similar interview with co-winner, Ray Lindsay, later in the summer during Fleetwood Mac's U.S. tour.

Photo By: *Metropolitan Photo Service, Inc.*

ROADIE-OF-THE-YEAR MEETS STARS OF "ROADIE"

Mike Sherrill (left), stage manager for Styx, proudly holds his Roadie-of-the-Year statuette, which was presented by *PERFORMANCE*. Here to share his triumph are Jim Cowen, *PERFORMANCE*'s New York Bureau Chief, and the stars of "Roadie," Art Carney, Deborah Harry, lead singer of Blondie, Meat Loaf, who plays Travis Redfish, the film's roadie, and Chris Stein, a member of Blondie. "Roadie" is an Alive Enterprises Production of an Alan Rudolph Movie

Performance Article

It was apparent that a dual winner was fabricated to satisfy the demands of the PR staff promoting the *Roadie* movie. This creative vote counting was the perfect way to recognize my profession.

149

The magazine did find me later that summer and their writer spent an afternoon with me at a show in Dallas close to their Ft. Worth offices. The interview covered my daily routine and walked through an array of the band's stage gear. Of special interest were my multi-guitar racks on both sides of the stage and in the dressing room. The ones for the *Tusk* tour were my third and newest version. I had built the first one in 1976 out of frustration with the uselessness of the flimsy single metal stands that were the only thing around. It wasn't complicated. Similar to a gun rack, it was a simple rectangular wooden stand with foam on the bottom for the guitar to sit on and individual slots with straps on top to hold the neck. It could hold 4 guitars standing side by side securely and safely. John McVie loved them and his approval was praise enough. My newest versions were more bulletproof and designed as a one-piece unit that could be folded up for storage in a road case. I made some for my friend Buggs with Tom Petty, and a couple for Jackson Browne, and Crosby, Stills and Nash, but that was the extent of my distribution.

A few years later I attended the National Association of Music Merchants (NAMM) annual convention in Anaheim. The four-day event was quite a party. It was closed to the public and access was available only to manufacturers of musical instruments and their vendors. However, every musician or roadie with an ounce of credibility in rock and roll was encouraged to attend the closed event. There was much wining and dining in an effort to gain the endorsement of industry insiders for anybody's product. Readily available was lots of free stuff and as well as the opportunity to run into fellow road wackos. I got a heads-up from a friend that there were copies of my guitar stand at the ULTRACASE booth.

Building custom road cases for traveling bands had become a respectable business and a handful of upstarts were challenging the industry leader, Anvil, for a chunk of the market. *ULTRACASE* of Anaheim was one of those competitors. I knew the owner, Dave Eastman, and had purchased a few of his cases in the past for Fleetwood Mac in support of his start-up company. The featured product at the *ULTRACASE* booth were knockoffs of the original "Lean It On A Lindsey" multiple guitar rack. A young hipster was out front with the display as I began to express my admiration for their "new" product. "What a great idea!" I exclaimed. "That's fucking genius. Who thought of that?"

As the earnest salesman proceeded to bullshit me about the company's brilliant designers and engineers, a familiar voice boomed from behind the back of the pipe and drape cubicle. "Shut up you dumb shit. That's Ray Lindsey."

I said, "Hi Dave," but the voice behind the curtain fell silent. I picked up a brochure and promised to call when he had more time to talk. Numerous phone calls to the office went unreturned. I wouldn't have a minded a piece of that pie. You're welcome, Dave.

Tuning room 1977- Roadie of the Year with roadie invention of the millennium

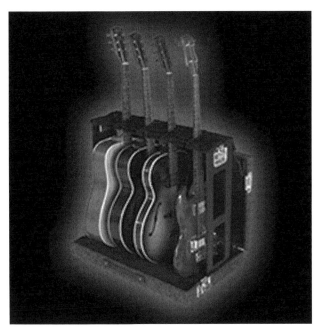

ULTRACASE homage to innovation and greatness

CHAPTER 21
MIRAGE ALBUM

Fleetwood Mac was a performing and touring powerhouse. I was working for and playing with the top band with the best sound and brightest lights selling out every show everywhere they went. What could go wrong? Well, apparently a few things. The largest issue was the profits not generated after all the expenses were paid. About a month after the *Tusk* tour was completed, there was a band meeting with accountants, lawyers, and all five band members. The news that they basically broke even was a grim revelation. Irving Azoff, Stevie's recently retained manager, laid down the new ground rules that had to be met before Stevie would participate in any further Fleetwood Mac endeavors. Basically, Seedy Management with Mick at the helm was to be dissolved immediately. The sacrificial lamb would be John Courage and the "Colonel" was let go.

There were no other bands of this magnitude with five equal members.

Springsteen was the "Boss" and his singular vision guided all of the decisions in and around his band.

The Stones were and always will be the domain of Mick and Keith.

The Eagles were clearly guided by Don Henley and Glenn Frey. They both shared a vision of fiscal success and responsibility before the band even started. Early on, they agreed that taking care of their money was as important as quality record making.

Fleetwood Mac's singers and songwriters had more visibility but at the end of the day it took all five to figure out how to come together and move forward on group issues. Band decisions usually focused on the creative side of things and business planning was a low priority.

When the band with new members Lindsey and Stevie first formed in 1975, they had no record, no tour and no money. They made an album in three months and toured the rest of the year. With minimal label support, no publicity, and only the money collected from the box office every night they began to build a dynasty on the strength of their live shows and support of their new record on FM radio. With just John Courage and a small road crew, these five strong, independent survivor personalities moved from one hard earned group success to the next. By the time *Rumours* hit big, all were convinced that they shouldn't argue with success. It would have been impossible for them to consider taking on a high-powered outside manager. There was no one on earth who could tell all five what to do and they had developed an aversion to being told "no." JC had no choice but to conduct business as usual and the shelf life on that practice had expired.

With Courage out of the picture, I was truly the last Mohican. Things would never be the same. The business ultimatums laid down at the tribal council had been directed at the touring side of the band's activities. Large scale restructuring would be implemented the next time we went on the road. In the meantime, the big machine was still going strong but with JC gone, there was even less direction than before. The music business cycle required fresh recordings and a new album release date. For the benefit of Mick's fragile financial state, a studio outside of the U.S. was sought out and Ken Caillat thought he had found the perfect recording destination in France.

The Chateau was located about sixty miles south of Paris in the tiny village of Hérouville. An authentic French chateau built in the eighteenth century, the property had been converted to a recording studio in the 1960's. Elton John, David Bowie, and others had recorded successfully there in the seventies and in 1981, it became Fleetwood Mac's next stop. Ernst & Whinney, the band's accounting firm, were the remaining supervising adults in the band business picture. I was their contact whenever they had billing questions about equipment purchases and now I was their contact for everything else. With no management offices or tour managers, it fell on me to organize the transfer of recording and band equipment from LA to France. With the help of David Bernstein and Rockit Cargo, I loaded a semi of gear into sea containers that were trucked to the East Coast and loaded onto a cargo ship headed for the port of Le Havre, France. After clearing French customs, all my stuff was reloaded into three small trucks and driven to Hérouville where I proceeded to take it all upstairs to the second floor studio. My partner, Tony, was in Africa with Mick and wouldn't show for another week, so second engineer Carla and myself finished setting everything up just as Ken, Richard, and the band arrived.

Le Chateau Recording Studio

The beautiful French farmlands and three hundred-year-old château were an idyllic setting but lacked the finer amenities found at the Ritz Carlton and The Village Recorder. Shared bathrooms and communal dining were quaint the first day and then not so much. The studio, even with all the extra gear we brought, was marginal and did little to improve morale. The new austerity ethos was off to a stumbling start.

Adding to the atmosphere of "why are we here?", was the presence of an other-worldly spirit that was maintaining a residence in his former abode. Frédéric Chopin was a Polish composer and virtuoso pianist. Born in 1810, he settled in Paris at age twenty-one and would spend the rest of his life living in France. He eventually ended up in Hérouville at the chateau and died there in 1849 at the age of thirty-nine.

It was accepted knowledge among the French staff that Chopin's ghost was quite comfortable spending his afterlife there. Our host engineer told us of the time he was working alone in the control room and had stopped the tape machine after listening back to a track. The sound of a pair of hands softly clapping in approval floated from the speakers. "Chopin" he shrugged.

Tony Todaro, Mick's drum guy, called bullshit and was convinced we were being wound up by the locals. When Tony formed an opinion, it was unshakable and non-negotiable. It was Mr. Todaro's belief that apparitions, foreign or domestic, were figments of misguided imaginations. Case closed.

The chateau was actually two buildings separated by a courtyard. One side was the studio and staff quarters. The other was our bedrooms, the kitchen, and dining room. We would work during the day in the studio and all gather in the dining room at supper time. Depending on how many bottles of wine were consumed, we would eventually wander back across the courtyard for a couple more hours of work. On one of these evenings, it was decided that we would get some drum sounds after dinner and Tony left to go back over to the studio side to change drum heads. I was about to join him when I was delayed by the opening of a nice bottle of French brandy. Time passed as did our enthusiasm for recording any drums. Our mellow was harshed by the explosive arrival of a red-faced Italian drum roadie. In my face with arms flying, Tony demanded to know when I had returned to the dining room. I pointed to the Armagnac and told him I never left.

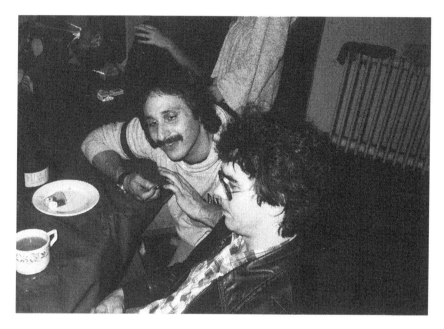

Tony Todaro

"Yes, you did! I heard you playing piano in the studio when I was downstairs working on the drums! I kept trying to talk to you but you just kept playing and wouldn't answer. I finally got pissed that you were ignoring me and went upstairs to find you. No one was at the piano. The room was empty. I yelled and yelled for you. Nothing. Then the room got really cold and I lost it. I ran all the way here."

Our French colleagues were nonchalant and unmoved by my partner's dynamic presentation.

"Ah ... Chopin" our cook Jacqueline said. "He likes to play games."

We all immediately jumped up and left for some ghost busting. Tony stayed with our hosts and the brandy. It was a week or so before he would return to the other side without a chaperone. For me, a larger mystery remained unsolved. How could Tony think Chopin's piano playing sounded like me?

Two months was about the most everyone could tolerate of the great French experiment. It was all too much like summer camp and the last thing the band needed was to be with each other day and night with no escape. They had been running on the adrenalin of success for a long time and fatigue was setting in. We had gone virtually nonstop for six straight years recording, rehearsing, and touring. The party with a soul was losing steam.

Larrabee Studio - Kells Jesse, me, John Stewart, LB and Ken Caillat

We headed back to LA in June 1981 and basically started over at Larrabee Studios in West Los Angeles. At least everyone could go home at night. When *Rumours* exploded, every night was like New's Years Eve with no regrets the next day. The festivities surrounding the making and touring of *Tusk were* just as robust but not as pain-free. The "day after" headaches were starting to be felt but you could still pull it together and get back in the game. Almost everything associated with the *Mirage* album and tour was a struggle and the hangover never went away.

Larrabee Studio

MIRAGE TOUR
SEPTEMBER 1982

01	GREENSBORO NORTH CAROLINA	GREENSBORO COLISEUM
02	ATLANTA GEORGIA	THE OMNI
03		
04	ORLANDO FLORIDA	TANGERINE BOWL
05	SAN BERNARDINO CALIFORNIA	US FESTIVAL
06		
07		
08		
09	LEXINGTON KENTUCKY	RUPP ARENA
10	NORFOLK VIRGINIA	THE SCOPE
11	PHILADELPHIA PENNSYLVANIA	THE SPECTRUM
13		
14	EAST RUTHERFORD NEW JERSEY	MEADOWLANDS ARENA
15	WORCESTER MASSACHUSETTS	CIVIC ARENA
16		
17		
18	INDIANAPOLIS INDIANA	MARKET SQUARE ARENA
19	DETROIT MICHIGAN	JOE LOUIS ARENA
20		
21		
22	EAST TROY WISCONSIN	ALPINE VALLEY
23	MINNEAPOLIS MINNESOTA	MET CENTER
24		
25		
26	OKLAHOMA CITY OKLAHOMA	THE MYRIAD
27	HOUSTON TEXAS	THE SUMMIT
28	DALLAS TEXAS	REUNION ARENA
29		
30	PHOENIX ARIZONA	COMPTON TERRACE

OCTOBER 1982

12	MEMPHIS TENNESSEE	MID SOUTH COLISEUM
13	BATON ROUGE LOUISIANA	LSU ASSEMBLY CENTER
14		
15	DENVER COLORADO	MCNICHOLS ARENA
16		
17		
18	IRVINE CALIFORNIA	IRVINE MEADOWS
19		
20	OAKLAND CALIFORNIA	OAKLAND COLISEUM
21	LOS ANGELES CALIFORNIA	THE FORUM
22	LOS ANGELES CALIFORNIA	THE FORUM
23		
24		
25	CEDAR FALLS IOWA	UNI DOME
26	LINCOLN NEBRASKA	DEVANEY SPORTS CENTER
27	ST. LOUIS MISSOURI	CHECKERDOME
28		
29	MOBILE ALABAMA	MUNICIPAL AUDITORIUM
30		
31	AUSTIN TEXAS	FRANK ERWIN EVENT CENTER

CHAPTER 22
MIRAGE TOUR

The *Mirage* album was finished in the summer of 1982 and a short tour was put together to support it. The band was still a huge draw and the brief U.S. run was a sellout before we left. This time, everyone was starting to retain their own managers and accountants in addition to the existing staff at Ernst & Whinney. All this careful overseeing didn't have any effect on our production or the band's performances. We were still the masters of our domain. The crowds were satisfied but the band was weary and starting to slow down. My personal petty needs were being met in the form of two additional songs to play guitar on. I now opened the show with the band playing *Second Hand News* from *Rumours* and *Gypsy* from the just released *Mirage* album. Both selections showcased my stunning ability to try to play as good as Lindsey did on the recording.

In spite of the presence of a new tour governing body, the band traveling party was conducting business as usual. Private jets, multiple limos, and luxury suites were all back. That stuff wasn't going away. The band was spending just as much money as they did on the *Tusk* tour and were fortunate to be offered a platinum opportunity to balance the books.

Steve Wozniak was a really rich guy. He and Steve Jobs were cofounders of Apple computers and were enjoying unimaginable success. Feeling the kids of the seventies had become obsessed with "me", Woz had a dream of celebrating and promoting the eighties as the "us" generation. His aspiration involved putting on a multi-day music festival/tech expo for himself and a few hundred thousand of his closest friends. This would be the precursor of what is now known as a "corporate gig"—private parties bankrolled by folks with plenty of their own cash to spend.

In the spirit of this entitled approach to concert booking, Wozniak made a list of his favorite bands and hired uber-promoter Bill Graham to stage the three-day show that would be known as the US Festival. The first day featured the Gang of Four, the Ramones, the English Beat, Oingo Boingo, the B-52's, Talking Heads, and The Police. Day two's lineup included Dave Edmunds, Eddie Money, Santana, The Cars, The Kinks, Pat Benatar, and Tom Petty. The final day opened up with the Grateful Dead followed by Jerry Jeff Walker, Jimmy Buffet, and Jackson Browne with Fleetwood Mac closing the entire show. When all was said and done, the first time promoter spent twelve million of his own money for the world's most expensive backstage pass.

To Fleetwood Mac, a million dollars for a two-hour set seemed like a good deal and the band happily accepted the party invitation. Now came the pesky details. When the US Festival offer came in, the sold out *Mirage* tour had already been planned and booked. On the schedule for Saturday, September 4, was an outdoor show for seventy thousand guests at the Tangerine Bowl in Orlando, Florida. We now had to figure out how to get everything to California for our appearance the next day, the fifth, to close the US Festival.

Lighting was already installed and our sound company, Clair Bros., was providing all the audio for the festival so that just left the issue of transporting the band's guitars, amps, drums, etc. from east coast to west coast overnight. The 737 chartered for us to carry band and crew had a cargo hold but wasn't large enough to bring all the stage equipment. My challenge was to go through every piece of gear we used and determine what components were irreplaceable and what could be duplicated with clones from LA. I had NEVER rented or substituted any of the band's equipment EVER. This was sacred territory and up until now, a non-negotiable piece of the Fleetwood Mac "no surprises" philosophy. Even though the band members had signed off on the concept of being "flexible", I feared that all bets would be off in the heat of battle. Nevertheless, we moved forward and put together a list of what we could replace and what we couldn't.

The temperature in Orlando on show day was in the nineties with seventy percent humidity. The band finished their set around ten p.m. and my crew and I separated the traveling pieces of equipment from the staying behind ones. The "to go" pile was loaded into a rental truck for the drive to the airport. Our charter plane was on the tarmac with all the cargo doors open and engines idling to keep the band and their entourage comfortable while we stuffed the belly with road cases. After a sleepless six-hour flight we landed at Ontario Airport in Southern California where Rockit Cargo was waiting to receive everything we pulled off the plane. The band party took off for their hotel and my crew and I followed the gear to Glen Helen Regional Park near San Bernardino.

Christie, Stevie and Lindsey

When we arrived, the crowd of three hundred thousand was settling in and preparing for a toasty day that would see the temperature climb to a hundred and ten degrees. At least it was a dry heat. My old buddy, Michael Huber from Westwood Music, was already there with the supplemental back line. A master of pulling rabbits out of the hat, Mike had put together an assortment of amps, speakers, and etc. that duplicated a good chunk of our touring package. The reverse engineering enabled us to cut down our total case count by a third and was the only way the show made it on the plane.

My guys and I then started the process of integrating the borrowed gear with the pieces that made the flight. The assembling of this jigsaw puzzle was all done on the back of the stage basking in the glow of the San Bernardino summer while the rest of the day's bands played in front of us. There would be no way to soundcheck and I was apprehensive about trying out a half of a stage of rental gear in front of three hundred thousand people. By the time I stepped on stage to play the opening chords of *Second Hand News,* I was ready for this to all be over. I was punchy from too little sleep and beat down by two days of too much heat. It was dark and the size of the crowd didn't sink in until the band was introduced and was met with the roar of a third of a million people. That was enough to squeeze out the remaining drops of adrenalin left in my pummeled carcass and rise from the ashes one more time. Two and a half hours later the band left the stage a million dollars richer and an after-show party of epic proportions ensued.

The tour went two more months on autopilot until the end of October and this time the band went home with cash in their pockets. My crew went their separate ways and I met the truck at our storage building in the Valley for the tour's last load in. I hired some local guys to help me pull it all out and put it away one more time. When we finished, I locked the door, set the alarm, and went back over the hill to Century City and the Ernst & Whinney offices to turn in my last envelope of tour receipts. Head accountant David Blum was waiting with longtime band attorney Mickey Shapiro.

Ken Caillat, me and Richard Dashut backstage Mirage tour

Clearly, something was up as I hardly ever saw these guys and never together. We were very possibly going to be discussing something besides my petty cash receipts. They got to the point and briefly explained that the band had given themselves a time out and all business was officially suspended until further notice. My services were no longer needed. They handed me my last paycheck and that was that. I left to find a quiet place to have a couple of Scotches and ruminate on the ramifications of no longer being employed. Oh well, we had a good run.

The fact that my send-off lacked a certain personal touch wasn't really surprising. The band's remarkable strength centered around the stunning power they generated when they played and sang together. Most everything else they tried to do as a group didn't work so well.

They needed to stop so their souls could catch up and just as unplanned as their beginning had been, so was this particular ending. I had been beside and between them the entire run. I had seen and heard it all. I wasn't happy about not working but it was time to put it to bed for awhile. The band's iron constitution had taken all it could take. The grief was trickling down into my world and something had to give.

★ ★ ★

It would only be a few months until I was back with Lindsey in the studio working on his next album *Go Insane.* A new future was born for everyone as they rocked back and forth between solo projects and Fleetwood Mac. Lindsey left the band in 1987 and returned in 1997. Christine retired in 1998 and un-retired in 2014 reestablishing the same lineup that came streaking out of the cosmos in 1975. The set list for the two-year world tour featured twenty-two of their finest tunes with nineteen of those from their initial years of unparalleled productivity.

For seven and a half years this unbridled force of nature created a body of music and performing persona that has retained it's authenticity for over forty years. It all started with a small machine and five people who preferred to do it their way.

Well it isn't for the money
And it's only for awhile
You stalk about the rooms
And you roll away the miles
Gamblers in the neon
Clinging to guitars
You're right about the moon
But you're wrong about the stars
And when you stop
To let'em know
You've got it down
It's just another town
Along the road

The Road
Danny O'Keefe

CHAPTER 23
LOVEGOD

Back in my early days when I started in the music business, nobody went on tour to get rich. It was a cool way to make some money but there wasn't really a feeling that a career was being pursued. Living large was the more immediate priority. Fleetwood Mac's surprise hiatus that began at the end of the *Mirage* tour in 1982 pushed me to confront new realities as gravity sucked me back down to terra firma. I had been getting a paycheck for seven straight years and needed to find new sources of income.

Rock and roll touring was now a firmly established business filled with big machines and I began a new adventure as an independent gun for hire guitar roadie. Between Fleetwood Mac and LB projects, I toured, teched and tuned with Stevie, Don Henley, Jackson Browne, Dan Fogelberg, Tom Petty, Donovan, Crosby Stills and Nash, Keith Richards and Def Leppard.

On July 2, 1991, I received a call from Prince production manager, Skip Johnson. He was looking for someone to handle Prince's guitars and stage electronics for his next world tour. Dallas Schoo had spent previous years in that position but left to take a full time gig with the Edge and U2. Dallas and I were old friends from his time working for Mac support band Firefall in the 70's and urged Skip to check on my availability. Turns out I was extremely available and Skip's opening salary offer made it difficult to play hard to get. The only downside was that he wanted me there the next day. He was vague about the urgency but I agreed to tie up my business at home in one day and fly out the day after.

Two days later on the 4th of July I traveled from LAX to Minneapolis and was driven to Prince Roger Nelson's purple playground in Chanhassen, Minnesota. Paisley Park, nestled in the farmlands surrounding the Twin Cities, was a one stop filming, recording and tour production facility. There were two 1990's era state of the art recording studios, a fully staffed 24 hour clothing design and tailoring department, dance rehearsal rooms, business offices, kitchens, hair and makeup salons, tech support shop and ample lounging spaces. The basement warehoused countless shelves of 24 track two inch tapes filled with music written and recorded by Prince as well as the entire inventory of every piece of gear he had used for performing. The ramp from the ground level parking lot to the lower level provided secure access to the owner's parking space located next to an elevator that traveled directly to the living quarters on the 2nd floor. There was also a 12,000 square foot soundstage that was used for filming videos and movies as well as functioning as a full production rehearsal room. It was large enough to accommodate the entire touring stage, lighting rig, projection screens and a sizable chunk of the Clair Brothers S4 PA system. Every inch of the building was always clean, shiny and fully stocked to be around the clock ready for any endeavor the commander in chief deemed appropriate. The man knew how to throw a party.

It was early afternoon Independence Day when Skip dropped me off at the soundstage. The building was empty as every employee of the Paisley Park complex and the Prince touring party was observing the number one American summer holiday with a day not at work. Rehearsals had been underway for months already and the immense room was crammed with at least one of every component ever used to put on a Prince show. In the center of the stage was an assortment of guitars, amplifiers, speakers and electronics that, when effectively combined, could deliver the mardi gras of noise known as the Prince guitar sound. I had until ten the next morning to get up to speed and dial in some sounds that the Purple One would find pleasing to play at the following day's rehearsals. Spicing up this scenario was a colorful under the radar back story involving the comings and goings of a handful of guitar wranglers brought in before me to be the new guy. For a variety of unexplained reasons, no one was working out and Skip was getting heat from the boss for not finding someone that knew the ropes.

The applicant prior to me became so disillusioned with his gig that he bought his own plane ticket home on a Friday night after rehearsal and disappeared without a goodbye note or phone call. From that point on, Skip was levied a daily fine until a suitable replacement was secured. Every morning Prince would call his production manager and ask if he had a roadie yet. Each day with no good news Skip was required to slide a $100 bill under the door of the business office. Gilbert, one of the personal managers, would retrieve the bill and return it to Skip later that day. Apparently, the c-note made that circular journey about ten times before I showed up.

I spent the rest of the day and most of the night on my own plugging in and playing with different combinations of the equipment that was in front of me. I thought getting something that sounded like "Purple Rain" would be a good start. After chucking out some over the top toys and simplifying the signal path, I was able to get his custom "Cloud" guitar and Hohner Telecaster copy to sound pretty Prince like. Round midnight, I shut it down and headed over to my room at the nearby Country Suites. I was back at ten the next morning and found the current band, The New Power Generation, in their places and ready to go. I tuned the two main guitars, placed them in stands in front of the amps and sat down in a folding chair by the monitor guy.

About 10:20, a perfectly coiffed high heeled man in a canary yellow jumpsuit walked wordlessly by me, strapped on the matching canary yellow Cloud guitar and proceeded to take his band on a 20 minute flight covering Sly Stone, Al Green, Jimi Hendrix and finally, James Brown. After everyone took solos in "Papa's Got A Brand New Bag", Prince dipped his shoulder and the blazing train of rock and soul from outer space screeched to a group stop on the one. So this is how they roll in Minneapolis.

Prince waved me over for our first get to know each other chat. In a quiet, low voice he said,

"The clean sound is boxy."

I walked back to his rack and dumped 500 cycles out of the 1/3 octave graphic equalizer on the clean side and sat back down. He strummed three times and looked up at me.

"That's good."

We had no further discussions the rest of the day as the band rehearsed new material for the tour. After about four hours, Prince set his guitar back in it's stand, walked past me and out the door. Band leader Levi called the rehearsal and that was it. Appearing next to me for the first time that day was Skip.

"Oh good, you're still here. Are you going to stay?"

I was handed an envelope with my per diem and the keys to a rental car. My employment had officially started.

The next few weeks of rehearsal went the same way every day. Prince would silently arrive at the soundstage in a new outfit and matching boots, grab a guitar and play with his band for the next four to eight hours. Our relationship was based on mutually ignoring each other. Except for asking me to make him a daily cup of tea - english breakfast with a little honey and milk - we had few conversations. It wasn't just me. He was a quiet guy and if a topic wasn't about the music he was immediately involved with, he wasn't interested. He reminded me of Lindsey. LB and Prince were six string virtuosos but didn't define themselves as just guitar players. They were also writers, arrangers and producers and their focus on the creative big picture carried more weight than their identity as a rock guitar god. Another similarity was their preference to do their experimenting with guitar sounds in the recording studio and not become distracted with gear tinkering when it was time to play live. It was obvious Prince would let me know if he had a problem and I was pretty confident he wasn't a fan of casual technical banter about cable impedance and amplifier biasing.

I really began to enjoy my new gig. This was a big machine firing on all cylinders. Prince had his fingers in EVERY detail and was not coy about letting anyone know exactly how he wanted something done. You knew where you stood with him and didn't have to second guess anything. The music was never ending and always funky, badass, soulful and impeccable. Before I showed up, he had spent a year training each of his musicians in the fine art of paying attention to Prince and they had collectively gained his trust. He was demanding with his band but they always delivered the goods.

In September, we took the party out to Los Angeles for the MTV Video Music Awards. Broadcast live from the Universal Amphitheater on the fifth, we opened the show with a seven minute version of "Gett Off" from the just released *Diamonds and Pearls* album. The presentation was a PG version of "Caligula" with a couple dozen g-stringed dancers humping while Prince sang, danced and played guitar. The set was comprised of 20' high flaming Roman columns surrounding the band's risers. Earlier in the day during the two hour sound check, the quick changing soldier of fashion directed the camera blocking in a knee length coat that covered his lacy stage clothes underneath. The continuous conveyor belt of fresh frocks was just part of daily life with Prince and it would be unheard of to see him wear the same thing twice. The song started with guitar, moved to dancing and finished up with a guitar solo. I made my place in the mosh pit at the front of the low stage for my cues to receive and later return his guitar to him. I was by myself during the closed dressed rehearsal in the afternoon, but at showtime, an SRO pack of MTV super fans pinned me in place. Host Arsenio Hall made the introduction as Prince entered with his band and guitar from the middle of the stage. His long coat from earlier in the day was gone as he stood three feet in front of me singing at his microphone. About two minutes into the performance, my Artist removes his guitar for the first hand off and gives it to me. It was at this time he turned to reveal his ass less trousers to me and the national live TV audience. In my short time in my current position, I had come to be not too surprised about anything my boss came up with. This time he got me. He smiled at me over his shoulder, winked and took off along the front of the stage, proudly displaying his princely posterior to one and all. I have to admit - the brother had one fine butt.

2001 MTV VMA Awards

The band's ability to musically turn on a dime was a key element in the NPG strategy for success. Every player was equally accomplished in their own right but they all had to keep themselves ready for the always coming next surprise. We would usually rehearse five to six days a week and started pretty regularly around ten am. It was anybody's guess what would be worked on until our leader arrived. The general theme was be ready for anything.

On one of these mornings, Prince walked on to the stage past the whole band over to the drum set. Drummer Michael Bland got out of the tractor seat he sat on to let the boss take his place. After watching Prince play a few bars of a steady greasy pattern, the big boned youngster nodded that he was ready, reassumed his position behind the kit and proceeded to mimic the swing perfectly. Next "P" grabbed Levi's blue hollow body and strummed a rhythm pattern that danced on top of the rock steady beat. He handed the guitar back and his musical director instantly cloned the part. The room was already percolating when Prince turned to his bass player. Standing in front of and facing the left handed playing Sonny, the composer placed his fingers on the fretboard of the bass guitar like he was playing a keyboard to show what he wanted. Even more impressive than that display was Sonny's ability to nail the pattern and instantly take off on his own. When Prince sat down at his piano and hit the keys, the notes filled the air above the rhythm section and we all heard the song's melody for the first time. The core four put it on a low flame and let it simmer on it's own for 20 minutes or so. There were smiling faces, tapping toes and nodding heads all around. It is a remarkable and warm feeling to start the day with soul drenching music so right that you forget you're at work. With lyrics already written, the band spent the next 2 hours putting the pieces together and locking it in. We took a lunch break while the horn section was called. At two o'clock, the session guys arrived and wrote out their charts as sung to them by Prince. By 5 o'clock, the entire piece had been arranged, rehearsed and made ready to record. We broke down the band equipment and wheeled it over to the studio where the gear was reassembled, miked up and tweaked for recording. Once levels were sorted out, the band returned to lay down the newly learned track. Somewhere close to midnight, Prince finished the mix and we all went home. All the tapes then made their way downstairs to the shelves that already held hundreds of other completed but unreleased Prince songs patiently awaiting their day in the sun.

His Royal Pick

The original plan of touring in the fall was pushed back to the following spring and the entire crew was kept on to rehearse away a sub zero Minneapolis winter. Depending on the weather, Prince would vacate for a week or two and leave us on our own. Levi would run the practice sessions while taking instructions over the phone. I used the time without my Artist to build the most bulletproof guitar rig I could think of. I had been on the scene for 7 months and my success at keeping Prince from fining Skip had afforded me some insider power. Basically I had a blank check for anything I felt was essential to the world of Prince's stage equipment. To minimize any distractions that might occur if a piece of gear went down during a performance, I built a duplicate electronics and speaker package that would be in play with the main system whenever Prince was playing guitar. Both units had their own dedicated inputs to the house and monitor system. Any component could fail in the "A" system and Clair engineers Dave Natale and Ed Dracoules would just open up their "B" set of inputs to access the identical guitar sound blasting in tandem from the supplemental gear. It was Prince worthy and a perfectly reasonable insurance policy to address the loaded question "what could go wrong?".

There was a lot of TV watching in my warm hotel room that winter and plenty of time to observe the various ways the natives dealt with the god awful cold. A major contributor to the lack of heat was a weather phenomenon known as wind chill. Growing up in Kansas, I was familiar with the effects that a 30 mph wind can have on already cold temperatures. It can take a temp in the teens and make it feel like ten below zero as it cuts through you like frozen knives. That was the minor leagues compared to the northern plains version. The condition was so extreme that the daily TV forecast included an advisory detailing the maximum minutes human flesh could be exposed before frostbite set in. This daily reminder of potentially fatal weather elements was usually delivered in a cheery broadcaster voice between the latest Gopher basketball scores and new chili recipes. I had developed a fondness for these hardy plains folk and was seriously considering relocating to the Twin Cities to secure long term employment but these numbing polar patterns could be a deal breaker.

A more humorous winter related event is an annual ritual that signals the coming of spring. Minnesota is known as the land of 10,000 lakes and the summertime has them filled with winter weary locals enjoying all the outdoor activities that water and sun can support. When the Canadian cold fronts return and put every single body of water back in the deep freeze, outdoorsy types take to the ice for some off season fishing. Everybody parks their cars on the frozen waterways and build little villages populated with heated huts to engage in some winter trolling. Holes are cut in the ice and bundled up anglers huddle next to camp stoves while dropping their lines into the nearly frozen lake below.

As an outsider not familiar with this enduring past time, I assumed this practice was another latitude driven reason to get out of the house. It appeared that alcohol was a factor as well. Towards the end of the arctic fishing season, an unofficial Russian Roulette based on anticipating the melting of the ice cranks up. The majority of seasoned sportsmen who have spent the winter on top of a frozen lake have packed up their campsites and headed home while the getting was good. These are the reasonable humans that will most likely return next year with all of their possessions. Remaining is a faction of rebels, holdouts and deniers that seek to challenge the thaw rate and unintentionally secure a slot on the evening news. Every year for a week or so, local TV reporters across the state stand on lakeside shorelines with a camera crew and interview a new pack of regretful midwesterners pointing to pickup truck sized holes in the ice behind them. Ah … tradition.

Springtime is when we finally assembled our troops, hardware and Princely visions to launch the *Diamonds and Pearls* tour. Our army of 60 plus started in Tokyo on April 3rd and ended up in Paris on July 12. Stadiums and arenas were sold out and filled to capacity at every stop. This was the size of tours Fleetwood Mac had enjoyed but the Prince version pimped it out to the next level. The Mac had a deep bench and divvied up the spotlight between 3 front people. They also pretty much stayed in one place once the show started. Prince carried the entire 2 hour plus show on his own shoulders and rarely stopped moving. Our show was a non stop festival with multiple stage levels and numerous entrance and exit points. We had a Broadway theatrical stage manager calling cues to coordinate set moves, dancer positions, pyro displays and the nightly flying of a bed with Prince and 2 ladies 30 feet over the heads of the crowd down front. Besides playing guitar, my Artist sang, danced and played piano using every square foot of the stage. Since only half of the show was with guitar, I too followed a script that detailed every stage position and song that required handing off an instrument or taking it back. Guitars and wireless microphones would also randomly come flying my direction when the owner felt inspired to see if I was paying attention. Final tally was no broken guitars but I did lose a microphone once that was launched from the other side of the stage and disappeared in the lights.

Towards the end of the European leg of our tour, Lindsey Buckingham and I crossed paths at a hotel bar in London where he coerced me to leave Paisley Park and come back to L.A. to help him put together his first solo tour. I really enjoyed working for Prince but my first loyalty was always to Lindsey. I had waited a long time for my #1 mentor and inspiration to step out on his own. Another factor in my decision was the cold hard fact that another Minneapolis winter was going to be tough to take. Lindsey had just finished his solo album *Out Of The Cradle* and wanted to put together a group with enough players to replicate live all the guitars and percussion that he put down in the studio. Enabling his 10 piece big band vision was the beginning of 17 more years with LB in his studio, on tour and back again to Fleetwood Mac. In September 2004, I worked my final gig with the Mac and began my transition to the once taboo world of television - or the "the dark side" as it is referred to by my music audio brethren.

My last Fleetwood Mac show Detroit September 2004

CHAPTER **24**
FURTHER ON UP THE ROAD

In the early days of rock and roll, television and movies had a simple way to deal with most music audio issues. Singers lip synced to a pre recorded track and the musicians pretended to play along. This was the kind of control that producers and directors were most comfortable with and the artists complied because, for the most part, they were just happy to be there. As the mid sixties started creeping in, rock music was becoming the backing track for independence, rebellion, confrontation and generally refusing to be told what to do. The buttoned down world of TV production was not an advocate for any of those things. Once you walked onto a soundstage, you were expected to surrender to the direction and ideas of any number of department heads and technicians following a finely detailed script. There couldn't have been a more contrary environment for the counter culture to be playing their tunes in. The controlled sanitized audio levels imposed were the hardest obstacles to overcome. Bad microphones, no monitors and neutered PA systems were the last straw in keeping most bands from playing ball. It took years for TV to get over their control issues and surrender to the new order. As with most things in show business, the sweet smell of big money began to motivate the powers that be to look inward and find a way to be better. They began to realize that the key to capturing a band at their best was to get out of the way and figure out how to adapt TV protocol to benefit the musician's production needs. An early industry development helping to initiate this transition was the arrival of the mobile recording truck.

Wally Heider was a large lumbering man obsessed with big band music and the recording of all the great artists of that genre. Besides his immense catalog of big band recordings, he built and ran iconic studios in San Francisco and Los Angeles that produced a hefty chunk of the best albums of the late sixties and seventies. In addition, Wally was also a pioneer in the mobile recording field. Beginning in 1958, he was the first to install studio quality recording gear in a truck and bring all the right stuff to an off site venue. His recording of Ray Charles at the Shrine in 1964 is just one of the many classic LP's he was responsible for in the early sixties. The music he captured for the movie *Monterey Pop* in 1967 prompted cinematographers to acknowledge that dedicated audio multi tracking would forever be an essential element of the filming and presenting of rock bands on the screen.

In the seventies, popular music had an incredible presence and was more than big business, it was part of the culture. Analog recording technology and expertise was at it's apex and was keeping pace with the amazing musical creativity of the times. The demand for enduring and sonically satisfying albums was huge. Instead of X – Boxes, almost every living room had a good set of speakers and one turntable. A constant stream of fresh studio albums were keeping the listening public blissed out but rock fans also loved their music live. The next best thing to being there was listening at home to records of their favorite band's concert tour.

The Wally Heider Mobile Recording trucks were the kings among the handful of specialty vehicles traveling the countryside taping for posterity every kind of band imaginable in their live native habitats. Compared to making albums in a brick and mortar studio, live albums were cheaper to produce and enabled the artist to give their fans a well-recorded well produced souvenir of their show.

It was only right that when the time came for Fleetwood Mac to record remotely that the Wally Heider mobiles would be employed. When we were recording *Rumours* in Sausalito, Heider alumni Ken Caillat booked the truck to put on tape Christine's grand piano for *Songbird at* Zellerbach Auditorium in Berkeley. In 1979 as the recording of the *Tusk* double album was winding down, we took the entire party out to Dodger Stadium for an afternoon of celebrated audio excess documented by the Wally Heider crew. Paul Sandweiss, Biff Dawes, Dennis Mays and Doug Fields manned the tape machines and microphones as the 112 member USC Trojan marching band was recorded on the famous ball field for their triumphant and regal arrangement for the album's title track. More, bigger and louder was never in better company.

On the ensuing tour supporting the *Tusk* album, the Helder truck and posse followed us all over the states filling countless reels of multi track tape with Mac shows that would become the *Fleetwood Mac Live album* that was later released in 1980.

The eighties and nineties saw the gradual evolution of television production priorities rising to the challenge of being less hostile to musicians. The once hated prospect of having to play on TV was being replaced with a new business reality. The costs of touring were skyrocketing and bands/management began seeking out broadcasting opportunities as a smart way to reach a huge audience with very little investment. Audio companies like ATK Audiotek in Los Angeles began to supply touring quality sound hardware and sound men to the production companies in charge of making the technical side of their TV shows successful. Most all the guys I knew that had worked at Wally Heider's eventually found a new home on "the dark side" bringing all of their live recording expertise to the small screen. After many years of wooing, I too eventually crossed over and joined forces with my loyal buddies from the road.

TV can be a complex and strange beast. I doubt that I would have landed there if there hadn't been a need for people familiar with the behavior patterns of the performing musician and their instinctual reluctance to keep things moving. Coupled with my compulsion to make things sound less crappy, I magically and ironically found myself with a career in television.

I love happy endings and my current place of employment is contributing greatly to that hopeful outcome. This is my eighth year in the music audio department of Conan O'Brien's late night talk show and there is not a better place on TV to be. A well oiled machine filled with smart creative people, every department is staffed with a healthy balance of skilled technicians and amiable knuckleheads. There are guitars and guitar players everywhere and laughing at the boss is not only OK, it's mandatory.

That's all I've got for now.

Stay tuned.

Peace.

I did my time in that rodeo
It's been so long and I've got
Nothing to show
Well I'm so plain loco
Fool that I am
I'd do it all over again

Mercenary Territory
Little Feat

May you be safe and well
May your heart be filled with loving kindness
May you live in peace
May you be free

Dedicated to the memory of

Bobby Lindsey
Kasey Alsbury
Judy Wong
John Courage

CREDITS

Waterfront Publishing
    Bill Gladstone
    Gayle Gladstone

Editor
    Kenneth Kales

Cover Design and Art Direction
    Christie Lindsey

Publicity
    Kaitlin Lindsey

Photography
    Ray Lindsey, Herbert Worthington, Neale Preston
    Bill Paustenbach, Sam Emerson, Paul Guthrie, Leo
    Rossi, Dave Richanbach, Kaitlin Lindsey and Ken D'Alessandro

Gratitude and Appreciation to Kathleen Weimer

Hey Mr.Music
You sure sound good to me
I can't refuse it
What to be
Got to be

Roots, Rock, Reggae
Bob Marley

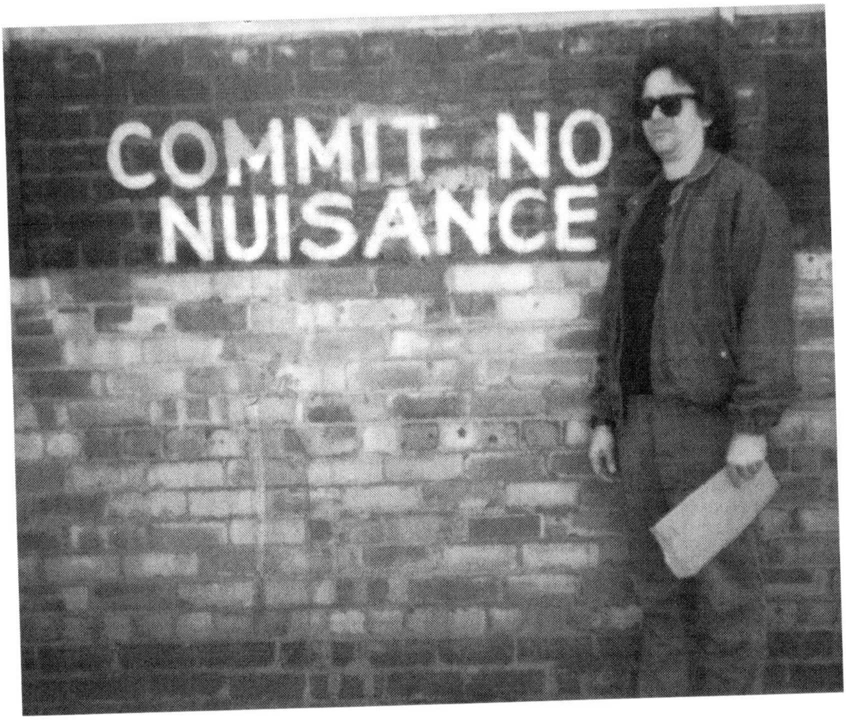
COMMIT NO
NUISANCE

37778890R00110

Made in the USA
Middletown, DE
02 March 2019